BURIED LIVES

The Enslaved People of George Washington's Mount Vernon

BY CARLA KILLOUGH McCLAFFERTY

HOLIDAY HOUSE / NEW YORK

The Publisher would like to thank Mary V. Thompson, Research Historian at the Fred W. Smith National Library for the Study of George Washington at Mount Vernon, for her expert review of this book; and Kimberly Wallace-Sanders, PhD, Associate Professor of American Cultural History and African American Studies, Emory University, for her thoughtful sensitivity evaluation of the manuscript.

Book design by Trish Parcell Watts
HOLIDAY HOUSE is registered in the U.S. Patent and Trademark Office.
Printed and bound in August 2018 at Hong Kong Graphics Ltd., China.
www.holidayhouse.com
First Edition

1 3 5 7 9 10 8 6 4 2

Library of Congress Cataloging-in-Publication Data

Names: McClafferty, Carla Killough, 1958- author.
Title: Buried lives : the enslaved people of George Washington's Mount Vernon / by Carla Killough McClafferty.
Description: First edition. | New York : Holiday House, 2018. | Audience: Ages 10 and up. | Audience: Grade 4 to 6.
Identifiers: LCCN 2016058471 | ISBN 9780823436972 (hardcover)
Subjects: LCSH: Slaves—Virginia—Mount Vernon (Estate)—Juvenile literature. | Washington, George, 1732-1799—Relations with slaves—Juvenile literature. | Slavery—Virginia—Mount Vernon (Estate)—Juvenile literature. | Mount Vernon (Va. : Estate)—Race relations—Juvenile literature.
Classification: LCC E312.17 .M394 2018 | DDC 306.3/62097341--dc23 LC record available at https://lccn.loc.gov/2016058471

Dedicated to the memory of my son,
Corey Andrew Killough McClafferty

CONTENTS

FOREWORD

I first met Carla Killough McClafferty over the telephone on the day she called to ask me for an interview related to her upcoming book, *Buried Lives: The Enslaved People of George Washington's Mount Vernon.* She'd contacted me because one of the women she writes about in the book is Caroline Branham, my fourth great-grandmother on my father's side. Her questions to me were aimed at learning what my family knew about my ancestor, who was an enslaved housemaid to the Washington family. Carla asked especially for information that would help fill the gaps in the records of Caroline's life story—a story that played out as Caroline stood in the shadows of the great and powerful.

I will never forget the conversation Carla and I enjoyed about eighteen months later, when we met face-to-face for dinner at a lovely restaurant in downtown Alexandria, Virginia. Mount Vernon historian Mary V. Thompson joined us, and over our meal Carla enthusiastically shared the journey she had taken in researching the life stories of the individuals she wanted to profile in her book. That journey has culminated in the publication of *Buried Lives*—a book that brings to light some of the life experiences of several of George Washington's enslaved people.

In these pages we find housemaids, seamstresses, cooks, and horse breeders, each portrayed as the individuals they were: people with a sense of personal authority that transcends the circumstances in which they found themselves. The Washingtons are viewed through the eyes of the enslaved community, as the reality of slavery at Mount Vernon is detailed in the daily business of maintaining status and sorting out duties that made the best use of the Washingtons' laborers. *Buried Lives* presents an excellent examination of class and privilege in the formation of this country—and it is also important because it opens a door to the presence of courage, daring, and ingenuity not commonly thought to exist in the strategies of enslaved people.

Whenever I've spent time at Mount Vernon, it has always given me pause to think that my ancestor once walked in the presence of so many great people. At any given time, visitors from America, the West Indies, and Europe—many of them political leaders—were received by the Washingtons. I wonder, though, how Caroline felt as she cared for the comfort of dignitaries such as the Marquis de Lafayette, who opposed slavery, and others who shaped world philosophies and laws. These people were brilliant in the light of their freedom. What about Caroline's freedom, and the freedom of the other people who labored alongside her? What did they feel as they heard about resolutions that would continue to inflict indignities on them, while at the same time securing the freedom and dignity of white Americans?

I have dedicated twenty-eight years to the research of my father's family, and have long felt that the people who served the needs of the First Family, including Caroline Branham, deserve to be known in their own right. After all, it was their labor that gave General Washington the freedom to leave his estate when necessary in order to develop the guiding principles and policies of our nation—and, for a time, to lead it. In my estimation, they, too, were first families of America who played a major role in its history.

While researching the lives of my ancestors, I've found that there is no way to describe the joy of finding gems of historical information that reveal the words, talents, hobbies, and accomplishments of family. We, the living, tell the tales of those who have died. Their place in history rests in how well we preserve evidence of their fortunes and miseries. The experiences and influences of our ancestors continue to shape us and surround us. But, like those who came before us, we must always find a way to push through and flower wherever we are planted.

ZSun-nee Miller-Matema
Founder of AFRIAsia:
The Intercultural Education Exchange/
Attitudes for America
Washington County, Maryland

Introduction

George Washington, the man who led the fight for American freedom, was a slave owner. At the age of eleven Washington inherited ten human beings, and he would own people his entire life. By the time Washington was born, African people had been enslaved in the Americas for hundreds of years.

According to Voyages: The Trans-Atlantic Slave Trade Database, maintained by Emory University, between the years 1501 and 1866 an estimated 12,521,300 Africans were forced onto slave ships that sailed to different destinations. Full ships set sail with their human cargo, who were shackled together in horrendous conditions belowdecks. Over the years, an estimated 10,702,700 people survived the voyage (almost 15 percent died), and of them, approximately 388,700 (3.6 percent) arrived in mainland North America—part of which would eventually become the United States. The majority (approximately 95 percent) were sold to slave owners in the Caribbean and South America, while approximately 8,900 (0.08 percent) were sent to Europe and about 155,600 (1.5 percent) were taken to other locations in Africa.

Those taken to North America were delivered to ports in both Northern and Southern colonies (which later became states). Abused and frightened, the men, women, and children who lived through the crossing were then taken to slave auction houses and put on public display. White potential buyers looked them over as if they were cattle—property to be bought and sold. At these public sales, African people were auctioned off and sold to the highest

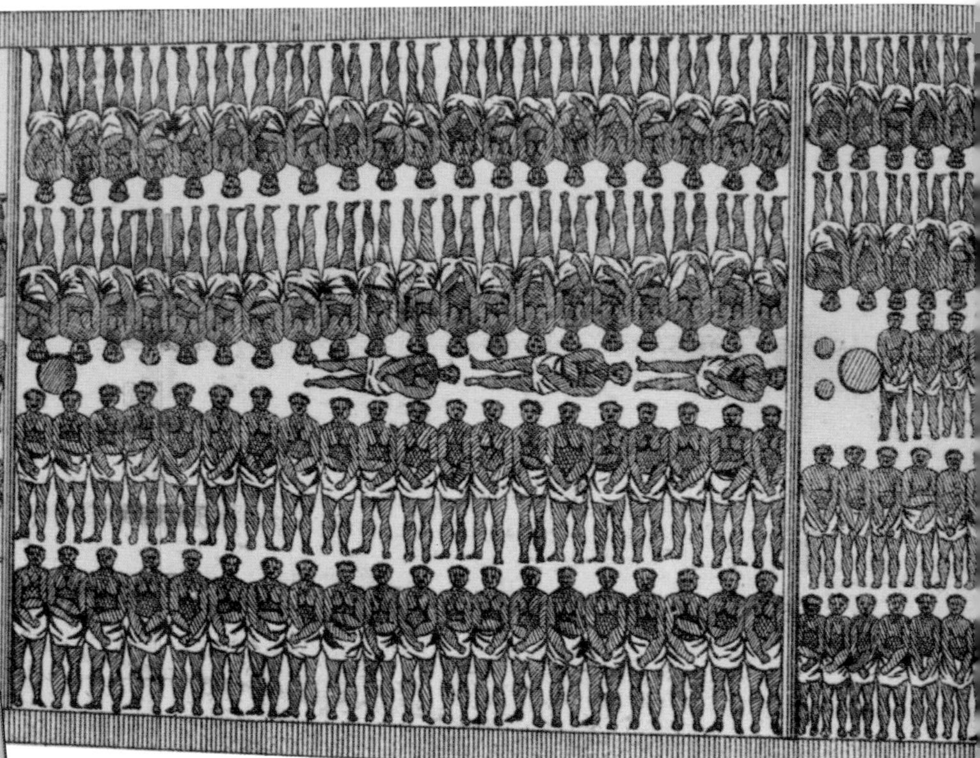

TOP and LEFT: Enslaved human beings were packed into ships as cargo during the transatlantic slave trade. This is a 1788 diagram of the British slave ship *Brookes* (also spelled Brooks). That year, the British government limited the number of enslaved people who could be transported on each ship based on its capacity, and the *Brookes's* limit was 454. However, the previous year, 609 enslaved people (about 349 men, 126 women, 91 boys, and 43 girls) were taken from west Africa and forced belowdecks on the *Brookes*. By the time the ship arrived in Jamaica where they were to be sold, 19 of them had died.

Abolitionists used this diagram to illustrate the horrific reality of slavery, including Thomas Clarkson, who had two models built of the *Brookes*. William Wilberforce, a British politician, used one of the models to show members of Parliament when he spoke out against the slave trade.

BOTTOM: This newspaper ad for a "Cargoe of fine Slaves" from Angola appeared in the *Virginia Gazette* on July 3, 1752. The sale took place in Yorktown, Virginia.

ADVERTISEMENTS.

June 30, 1752.

Juſt arriv'd in York River, *from* Angola,

THE Ship *Molly*, Captain *Iſaac Lane* with a Cargoe of fine Slaves, the Sale of which will begin at *York* Town, on *Monday* the 6th of *July*, and at *WeſtPoint*, on *Wedneſday* the 8th; and be continued there 'til all are ſold.

N. B. She is an entire new Ship, and will take in Tobacco at 6 *l. per* Ton, with Liberty of Conſignment to any Merchant in *London*: Notes may be delivered to the Captain on Board, and at the adjacent County Courts, or to

Nelſon, Tucker, & Company.

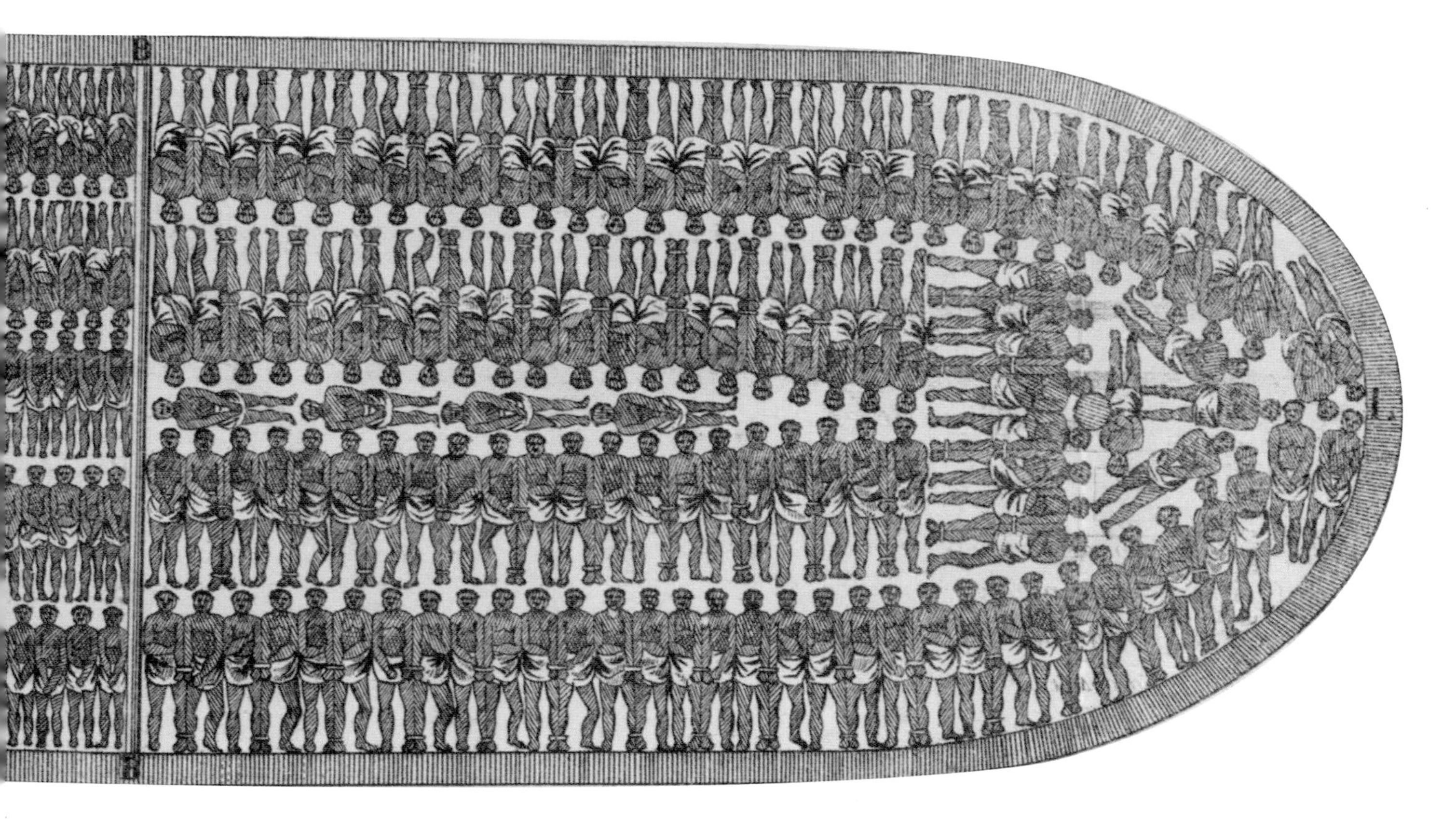

bidder. From that point on, they were the permanent property of the one who purchased them.

The buying and selling of human beings in this way is called "chattel slavery." Enslaved people were considered chattel—the personal property—of the one who owned them. Like any other type of property, they were bought, sold, traded, rented, and inherited.

Regardless of whether a person was captured in Africa and brought to the colonies or was born into slavery in the Americas, he or she was forced into servitude. No one chose to be enslaved.

That certainly held true for the people who were enslaved on George Washington's Virginia plantation, known as Mount Vernon.

The title of this book, *Buried Lives,* refers to the people George Washington enslaved in two ways. The first way is that while Washington's life is well documented, the compelling lives of the people he owned, and the valuable role they played in the history of America, are largely buried under layers of time and history. This book seeks to shed light on some of these life stories.

The majority of enslaved people in America were not permitted to learn how to read and write. A few who lived at Mount Vernon could, but unfortunately none of them left a written record of their lives. Still, information is known about the enslaved community at Mount Vernon because a wide variety of historical documents, written by George Washington and others, exist that reveal details about their lives. These primary source documents are the foundation of my research for this book.

The second way this book's title refers to the enslaved community of Mount Vernon is more literal. It concerns the final resting place of those who are buried there.

Two very different burial sites exist on the grounds of the former plantation. In life, the Washington family and the people they owned were worlds apart in their manner of living—and in death, the same holds true for their places of interment. George and Martha Washington each lie in a marble sarcophagus within a brick tomb. A short distance away, in the slave cemetery, graves are unmarked and their exact locations unknown.

But that is about to change. In 2014, archaeologists at Mount Vernon began a survey to reveal the location of each grave in the cemetery. It is their hope that this effort will, in part, help to connect the present to the past lives of the people buried there.

Of the hundreds of African Americans who worked at Mount Vernon, this book focuses on six people specifically: William Lee, Christopher Sheels, Caroline Branham, Peter Hardiman, Oney Judge, and Hercules. I've written about their lives and environments as accurately as possible. While there is much we can never know about their histories, what we do know speaks to us loud and clear.

The lives of the people in this book were intertwined with the life of George Washington, and vice versa. Nearly everything Washington did—where he went, the decisions he made, and in some respects what he accomplished—affected the life of every man, woman, boy, and girl who lived and served at Mount Vernon. And their forced labor—every meal cooked, every chamber pot emptied, and every crop harvested—affected the life of George Washington, because his lifestyle relied on the institution of slavery.

Washington was born into a slaveholding family. As a boy, he probably didn't question whether slavery was right or wrong—it was part of life as he knew it. He likely didn't know people who held anti-slavery beliefs until he was in his forties and became commander in chief of the Continental Army. It was then, during the Revolutionary War, that his friends John Laurens, Alexander Hamilton, and the Marquis de Lafayette spoke out against slavery. Because of the respect and admiration Washington had for these men, he listened. Slowly, Washington's view of slavery began to change.

At the start of the war, Washington and the Congress excluded African American men from enlisting in the army. However, when the army needed more soldiers, they were allowed to enlist and fight in all-black units. Then Washington put an end to segregated units and ordered white and black soldiers to serve side by side. After Washington's integrated Continental Army disbanded at the end of the American Revolution, it would be more than 170 years before full integration took place again in the United States military.

After the war, Washington's views had altered to the point that he wanted slavery to end. In a letter to John Mercer in 1786 he wrote that it was "among my first wishes to see some plan adopted, by the legislature by which slavery in this Country may be abolished by slow, sure, & imperceptable [sic] degrees."

But while this was Washington's private view, he did not publicly speak out against slavery, nor did he use his immense power and influence to work toward its abolition.

He was not unlike his successors in that regard. George Washington was neither the only founding father nor the only president of the United States who owned other human beings. Twelve presidents enslaved people at one time or another during their lives, including Ulysses S. Grant, the famous Union general of the Civil War, and Thomas Jefferson, author of the Declaration of Independence. After Jefferson's death, 130 of the people he owned were sold at a public auction to pay some of his debts.

In contrast to Jefferson and other Founding Fathers who were lifelong slaveholders, George Washington eventually drew up a will instructing that the men, women, and children whom he owned were to be freed upon his and his wife's death. Near the end of his life, he wrote, "The unfortunate condition of the persons, whose labour in part I employed, has been the only unavoidable subject of regret."

His decision would affect the people highlighted in this book to varying degrees.

AUTHOR'S NOTE

Most enslaved people during this period, regardless of where they lived, had a first name only. In this book, I refer to individuals at Mount Vernon by their first names when they did not have a last name or their last name is unknown. I use family names for the people who are known to have had one. In the case of Caroline Branham, I use her first name throughout most of the book because she did not use the family name of Branham until after she left Mount Vernon.

The spelling of names is inconsistent in the eighteenth-century documents I consulted during my research. In my writing, I chose one spelling for a name and used it throughout. However, when a name with an alternate spelling appears within quoted material, it is left as originally written. The same is true for misspelled words that fall within quoted material; they are left as originally written.

CHAPTER ONE

William Lee

William Lee, a sixteen-year-old African American boy, was for sale. It was 1768, and Mrs. Mary Smith Ball Lee wanted to sell him after the death of her husband, Colonel John Lee. In an estate sale of sorts, a thirty-six-year-old Virginia planter named George Washington bought William Lee (sometimes called Will or Billy). The price was £61, 15 shillings. That was about the same amount of money it would take to buy four good horses. Washington also bought Lee's younger brother, Frank Lee, for £50.

William and Frank Lee were called mulattos, a European term that had been in use for centuries to describe a biracial child born of a white parent and a black parent. The term stems from the word "mule," which means the offspring of two different species—a female horse and a male donkey. The Lee brothers' mother was an African American woman, and their father was a white man.

When an enslaved woman had a baby, the child was born into slavery. It didn't matter if the father was enslaved, a free black man, or a white man. Even if the master of a plantation fathered the child, the baby was still enslaved. The child was owned by whomever owned his or her mother. William and Frank both took the last name Lee—that of their former master. This may indicate who their father was.

The Lee brothers were taken to Mount Vernon. Many enslaved biracial men and women at the time labored in the fields. But like most other slave owners of the day, Washington tended to choose biracial people to serve inside the house. William Lee began working inside the house immediately and became Washington's valet. About three years later, his younger brother Frank was also assigned duties in the house.

Since William Lee worked as his master's valet, the family and their visitors would often see him. This meant that William Lee would be properly dressed. Suits, coats, and leather breeches were made and mended for him, and spatterdashes (spats) were ordered to protect his shoes and stockings.

Lee had more clothes, and nicer clothes, than most other people who worked elsewhere on the plantation, whose basic clothing was minimal. Every year, each enslaved African American man received one wool jacket, one pair of wool breeches, two linen shirts, one pair of linen breeches, and one pair of shoes for winter. If their assigned duty required them to wear stockings, they were given two pair. Each enslaved African American woman received one wool jacket, one wool skirt, two linen shifts, one linen skirt, one pair of shoes for winter, and one pair of stockings. Enslaved children got fewer clothes than the adults.

Lee's responsibility as valet was to take care of George Washington's personal needs. He was always near his master and thus spent an enormous amount of time with Washington. He cared for his master's clothes and laid them out each day. Once Washington had shaved and dressed himself, Lee helped him style his hair. In the current fashion, Lee brushed Washington's chestnut-colored hair back from his face, braided it, and fastened it with a silk ribbon. If the occasion called for a more formal look, Lee would powder his master's hair by smearing it with pomade and then using a puffer to apply white powder.

When the Washingtons had guests at Mount Vernon, the visitors often stayed for days, or even several weeks at a time. One of Washington's and his guests' favorite pastimes was foxhunting. On the day of a hunt, long before the sun rose over the Potomac River, Lee laid out his master's sporting clothes: a linen shirt, scarlet waistcoat, blue coat, buckskin breeches, tall boots, and velvet hunting cap.

Then, when dawn broke, William Lee no longer worked as a valet. The stout, muscular man then served as a huntsman. In a hunting party, the huntsman was responsible for taking care of the dogs and communicating with the hunters using a hunting horn.

Washington was considered by many to be the best horseman of his time. Lee was just as fearless on horseback when following the pack of barking, howling hounds. With his horn on his back, Lee leaned low over his horse, Chinkling, as he ran at full speed through the tangled woods.

Over the years, while attending to his master's needs, Lee likely heard Washington's conversations about the political unrest in the American colonies. In 1773, trouble was brewing in Boston, Massachusetts. To protest the tea tax, colonists crept onto ships in the harbor and hurled 340 chests of tea into the water in what became known as the Boston Tea Party. The British government was furious at this deliberate defiance and destruction of valuable property. King George III expected the citizens of Boston to pay for the tea they ruined. The colonists refused. The British government passed laws intended to force them into submission. The new laws forbade town meetings, put Boston under the military control of the British army, and closed Boston Harbor. In England the laws were called the Coercive Acts. But the American colonists called them the Intolerable Acts.

Although these acts were directed at the city of Boston, Massachusetts was not the only colony to consider them intolerable. Many people in each of the thirteen colonies were angry and fed up with the British government. In 1774 they called for a meeting of colonial leaders in Philadelphia, a meeting which later became known as the First Continental Congress. When Washington trotted away on his horse from Mount Vernon as a delegate from Virginia, the most powerful colony, William Lee was with him.

By the next year it was clear that war with England was coming. Once more, delegates were called to Philadelphia for the Second Continental Congress. Again, Lee saddled up to accompany his master to Pennsylvania. When they left that day in 1775, neither Lee nor his master knew that they would not see home again for over six years.

~

Once in Philadelphia, George Washington was chosen to be the commander in chief of the Continental Army. Lee traveled with him to Cambridge, Massachusetts, when he took command of his troops. Lee and General Washington lived in a beautiful three-story house near the Harvard campus that doubled as Washington's military headquarters. Just as he did in Virginia, Lee took care of his master's personal needs there.

An event that occurred on the Harvard campus that year gives us a fleeting glimpse of William Lee as General Washington's constant companion. Israel Trask later wrote about what he saw as a ten-year-old boy while working as a messenger and army cook in 1775, when troops from both Northern and Southern colonies were pouring into Cambridge to form the Continental Army.

Snow covered the ground that early winter day. Nearly a hundred riflemen from Virginia had just arrived and were looking around the Harvard campus. They encountered troops from New England, who teased the Virginians about their rustic clothes. A few threw some snowballs at the Virginia troops. A few Virginians threw snowballs back. Within five minutes the men had stopped throwing snowballs and started throwing punches. Soon about a thousand men were in an all-out fistfight.

At that moment General Washington arrived with William Lee right behind him. Trask wrote that he "saw [General Washington] and his colored servant, both mounted. With the spring of a deer, [Washington] leaped from his saddle, threw the reins of his bridle into the hands of his servant, and rushed into the thickest of the melee, with an iron grip seized two tall, brawny, athletic, savage-looking riflemen by the throat, keeping them at arm's length, alternately shaking and talking to them."

~

The only known reference to William Lee having a family of his own at Mount Vernon comes from a letter penned during the war by Lund Washington, a distant cousin who was managing Mount Vernon during the general's absence. On December 30, 1775, Lund wrote Washington, "If it will give Will any pleasure he may be told his wife and child are both very well." Nowhere else are this wife and child mentioned in the historical record, and it is unknown what happened to them.

However, during the Revolutionary War, Lee met a free black woman named Margaret Thomas. For the first two and a half years of the war, she sewed and washed General Washington's clothes and Lee's too. Because Thomas was one of the working women who followed army headquarters when it moved from place to place, Lee and Thomas would have seen each other continually around the military camp. Eventually they married, though no one knows when. After working for Washington's headquarters, Margaret Thomas Lee moved to Philadelphia.

As he had at Mount Vernon, Lee wore fine clothes during the war. General Washington wanted Lee and the enslaved man

This first-person historical interpreter is wearing a modern recreation of the livery worn by William Lee and other enslaved men including carriage drivers, butlers, and waiters who would have been seen by Washington's guests.

who cared for his horses to wear livery, special uniform-like clothes. Having his property dressed in livery for all to see communicated Washington's wealth, good taste, and social class without a word. On May 1, 1777, Washington wrote to Captain Caleb Gibbs, the commander of his Life Guard (bodyguards), ordering him to obtain all the supplies needed to have livery made for Lee. Washington knew exactly how he wanted the livery to look, and requested the following: "two Waistcoats, and two pair of Breeches—the Coats may be made of a light colourd cloth of any kind, lined with red Shalloon [lightweight wool]—a bit of red Cloth for capes, or Collars to them. Buttons & every kind of trimming must be sent, as nothing of the kind is to be had here."

During the war, Lee continued to serve as Washington's valet but had other responsibilities too. One of them was to keep Washington's papers safe when the army moved its headquarters from place to place. General Washington wrote thousands of pages of notes and letters containing information such as battle plans, maps, and communications with officers and spies. Lee was responsible for protecting the most important written information about the Continental Army.

He was also expected and trusted to keep secrets. Working as General Washington's valet meant that Lee likely heard everything Washington heard during the Revolutionary War—and was privy to most every secret of the Continental Army. Lee probably knew the strengths and weaknesses of each officer, the details of every battle plan, the number of troops and their location, how many cannons were available to them, and when their supplies of food and clothing were running low.

It was common knowledge that the British army promised freedom to any enslaved person who volunteered to join their ranks. If William Lee had tried to slip away to do that, he could have shared vital military secrets with the British. Serving in their army might have been his opportunity to escape a life of slavery and become a free man. But William Lee kept the secrets of the Continental Army, and stayed with the man who owned him.

William Lee protected General Washington's papers throughout the war. This is one of the trunks he moved every time Washington's headquarters relocated. Washington bought this secondhand trunk from a Boston merchant in April 1776.

The war continued. A few written descriptions survive that give us a glimpse into William Lee's life during this time, and how he was regarded by others. George Washington Parke (G.W.P.) Custis, grandson of Martha Custis Washington, recounted a description he likely heard as a child, of Lee during the 1778 Battle of Monmouth: "The servants of the general officers were usually well-armed and mounted. Will Lee, or Billy, the former huntsman, and favorite body-servant of the chief, a square muscular figure, and capital horsemen, paraded a corps of valets ... to an eminence crowned by a large sycamore-tree, from whence could be seen an extensive portion of the field of the battle. Here Billy halted, and, having unslung the large telescope that he always carried in a leathern case, with a martial air applied it to his eye, and reconnoitered the enemy."

The following year, at Middlebrook, New Jersey, army surgeon James Thacher wrote about William Lee in his journal. Thacher described a day when Washington inspected his troops while accompanied by a group of Native American chiefs. Thacher wrote that the general "with his usual dignity, followed by his mulatto servant Bill, riding a beautiful gray steed, passed in front of the line, and received the salute."

~

One of Washington's bodyguards, Uzal Knapp, remembered William Lee in 1780. Washington, his officers, and their wives attended a Christmas dinner, and Knapp recalled, "Old Billy, Washington's body-servant, whose head appeared like a bunch of white sheep's wool, was the chief waiter on that occasion and moved with great dignity." Although this guard recalled "old Billy" with white hair, Lee was only about twenty-eight years old. Perhaps his hair was prematurely gray, making him appear older than he actually was.

In 1781 General Washington ordered his army to Yorktown, Virginia, where he would face his old enemy General Charles Cornwallis in battle. Again and again throughout the war, the armies of Washington and Cornwallis had fought each other. This time, as Washington's army moved south toward Yorktown, it would pass near Mount Vernon.

For the first time in six long years, war-weary Lee and his master were home. Lee's family and friends were surely just as happy to see him as Washington's family was to see the general. But they stayed only a couple of days, just long enough to make plans for the battle ahead.

General Washington and his commanders, including Alexander Hamilton, John Laurens, and the Marquis de Lafayette, led the fight against the British. As soon as Washington saw that his troops had the victory, he called to Lee, "Billy, hand me my horse."

The brutal battle of Yorktown was the

Many historians think that the figure on the right is William Lee in this 1780 portrait of George Washington by John Trumbull.

turning point of the war and the last major battle, but the fighting wasn't over for another two years. The American Revolution officially ended on September 3, 1783, when the Treaty of Paris was signed. General Washington resigned as commander in chief of the Continental Army on December 23 of that year. At that point, all George Washington wanted to do was go home. William Lee must have felt the same.

Snow was falling that Christmas Eve, 1783, when Lee and his master rode their horses up the path at Mount Vernon and saw the mansion. They were home at last. Lee had been by his master's side through eight grueling years of war. Under the command of General Washington, America had gained its freedom.

William Lee had not.

~

With the war behind them, Lee asked Washington to make arrangements for his wife, Margaret Thomas Lee, to come to Mount Vernon. Washington apparently didn't like the woman, but his appreciation for Lee's service outweighed his feelings about her. On July 28, 1784, Washington wrote to Clement Biddle, who had been one of Washington's officers during the war:

"The Mulatto fellow William who has been with me all the War is attached (married he says) to one of his own colour a free woman, who, during the War was also of my family—She has been in an infirm state of health for sometime, and I had conceived that the connection between them had ceased—but I am mistaken—they are both applying to me to get her here, and tho' I never wished to see her more, yet I cannot refuse his request (if it can be complied with on reasonable terms) as he has lived with me so long & followed my fortunes through the War with fidility.

"After promising thus much, I have to beg the favor of you to procure her a passage to Alexandria either by Sea, by the passage Boats (if any there be) from the head of Elk, or in the Stage as you shall think cheapest & best, and circumstances may require—She is called Margaret Thomas als Lee (the name which he has assumed)."

In the end, Lee and his wife Margaret do not appear to have been reunited. No record exists that indicates she ever arrived at Mount Vernon. Washington's letter mentioned that she was not in good health. Perhaps she was too sick to travel, or died before she could make the journey. It may never be known why Margaret Thomas Lee didn't join her husband.

~

The war made George Washington world famous. Visitors, many of them total strangers, arrived at Mount Vernon to see him and his home. One of them was Elkanah Watson, a man from New England who dropped by on January 23, 1785. During Watson's two-day stay, he wrote in his journal that Washington was "revered and beloved by all around him," and that those who served him "seemed to watch his eye, and to anticipate his every wish; hence a look was equivalent to a command. His servant Billy, the faithful companion of his military career, was always at his side. Smiling content animated and beamed on every countenance in his presence." This is Watson's perception of how Lee and the others in the room felt about Washington. It is impossible to know what they really thought.

While Watson observed that the enslaved people at Mount Vernon diligently served Washington, he also recorded an incident that indicated to him that Mount Vernon's master was considerate of them at times. Watson wrote that when he went to bed for the night, he started coughing and couldn't stop. In a while, Watson heard someone at his door and "to my utter astonishment, I beheld Washington himself, standing at my bedside, with a bowl of hot tea in his hand." Washington could have called for one of the enslaved servants to take Watson some tea. Watson considered his actions a "trait of the benevolence and private virtue of Washington."

Of the constant stream of visitors that stopped by Mount Vernon, some stayed for dinner, while others, like Watson, stayed the night or several nights. No matter the length of their stay, they all enjoyed the warm hospitality of the Washington family. But it was the men and women owned by the Washingtons who cooked their meals, made their beds, cleaned their rooms, washed their clothes, and emptied their chamber pots.

Washington did not let visitors to his home interrupt the work that needed to be done on his plantation. Even though William Lee was Washington's valet, he also labored in other capacities. On April 2, 1785, Lee was working with his master to survey some land. At some point, Lee fell and broke his kneecap. Washington wrote in his journal that Lee was in such pain that it was "with much difficulty I was able to get him to Abingdon, being obliged to get a sled to carry him on, as he could neither Walk, stand, or ride." (Abingdon was the plantation home owned by Washington's late stepson, John Parke [Jacky] Custis. Today the site is on the grounds of Reagan National Airport.) Lee's broken knee probably caused him a lot of anguish and possibly a limp. Nevertheless, he continued as Washington's valet in spite of his injury.

Most guests at Mount Vernon didn't mention the names of specific enslaved African American people in their accounts, as Elkanah Watson did in his journal. But countless guests wrote specific details about Mount Vernon and their world-famous host, George Washington. In these writings, visitors likely never considered that most of what they saw and experienced was the direct result of the work of those who were enslaved. For example, when Robert Hunter visited Mount Vernon in November of 1785, he noted what Washington was wearing when they met. Washington had just returned from his daily ride around his farms and was wearing the clothes Lee would have prepared for him that morning: "plain blue coat, white cassimere waistcoat, and black breeches and boots." When his master returned, Lee would have had his dinner clothes ready and waiting for him to change into.

Dinner was at three o'clock. Fifteen minutes beforehand, one of the enslaved men or women serving in the house rang the dinner bell. When Washington appeared for the meal, Lee had dressed and powdered his hair and he had "a clean shirt on, a new plain, drab coat, white waistcoat, and white silk stockings."

Strangers, acquaintances, and friends all visited Mount Vernon. On June 20, 1786, Washington wrote to his old friend David Humphreys to say that when Humphreys visited the plantation, he didn't need to bring his own horses or "servant as your old acquaintance Will (now fit for little else) can whiten your head, & many idlers about the House can blacken your shoes." In this letter, Washington's callous remarks seem to indicate that he believed his enslaved people never worked hard or long enough. His comment about William Lee being "fit for little else" likely refers to the fact that Lee's knee injury prevented him from doing many of the tasks he'd done before.

Even though fulfilling his duties with a bad knee must have been challenging, William Lee continued as Washington's valet—and did the same for visitors, caring for their clothes and shoes, helping them dress, and powdering their hair.

~

Even as the number of visitors increased, Washington's life as a gentleman farmer slowly returned to normal after the war. But at the same time, he was growing more and more concerned about what was happening in the life of the newly formed nation.

By 1787 the Revolutionary War had been officially over for four years. To win independence from England, the thirteen American colonies had banded together to fight a common enemy. Once they were free, the colonies became thirteen states. Together they were one country, the United States of America, but they were only loosely tied together by a set of laws called the Articles of Confederation. There was no central government. People cared only for the issues that directly affected their state, and were uninterested in the well-being of the other states.

Because each state was independent, it was unclear how to solve the questions facing the struggling young nation. Who would pay back the money that was borrowed to

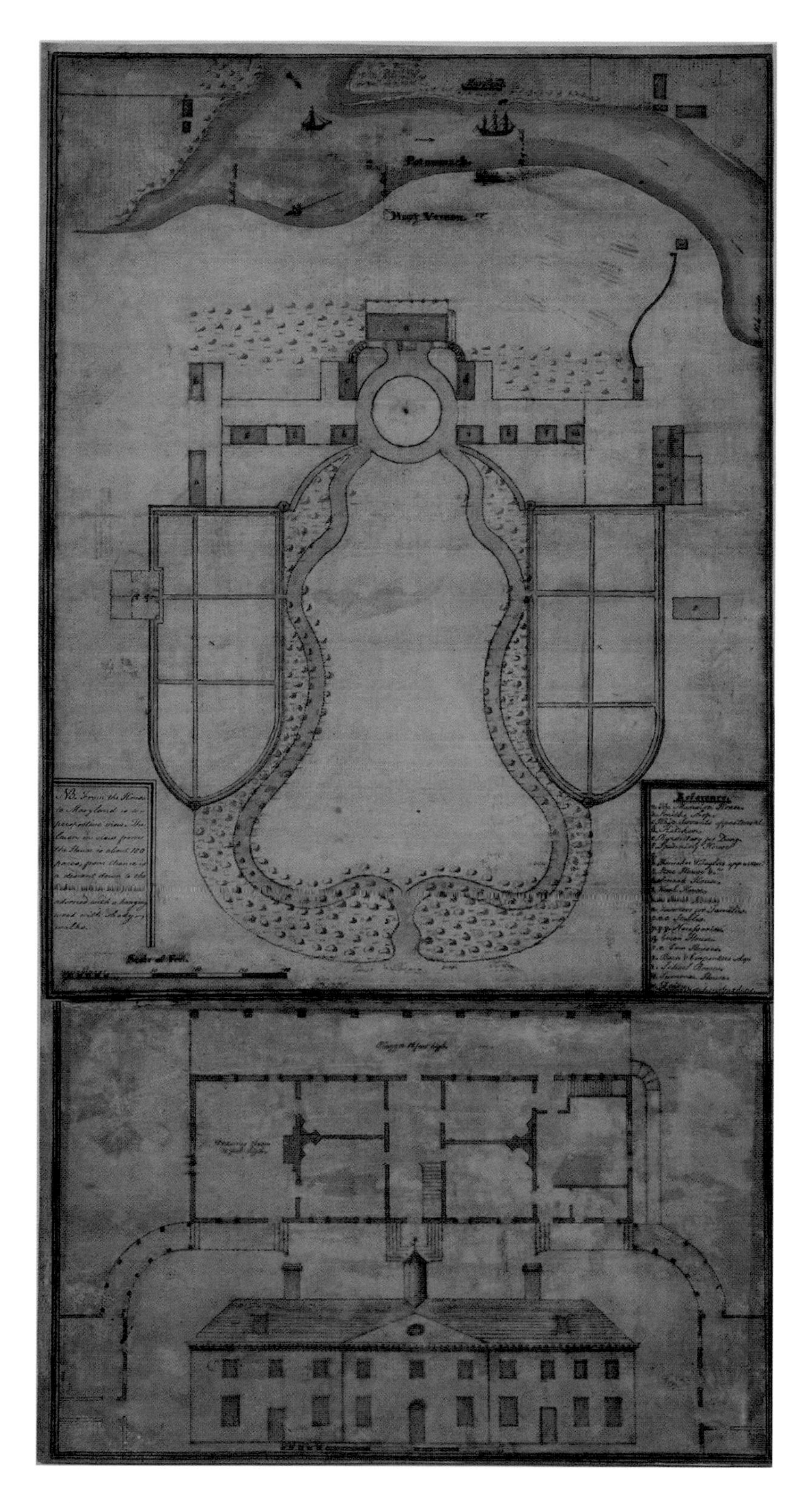

After the war, Washington worked toward improving his estate. During the summer of 1787, while George Washington and William Lee were away at the Constitutional Convention, Samuel Vaughan visited Mount Vernon and drew this detailed map of Washington's home and gardens.

fight the war? Would the rights of each state be more important than the rights of the nation? Which states would control navigation on the nation's rivers? What would happen as people moved into the wilderness that lay to the west of the states? Would slavery continue to be legal in every state?

If the newly united states were going to move forward as one nation, these and many other issues had to be addressed. New laws had to be adopted to govern the whole country. A new form of government had to be created. To hammer out the details, delegates from each state planned to gather in Philadelphia.

George Washington was one of Virginia's delegates. So once more, William Lee mounted his horse to follow his master north—this time, for what would become known as the Constitutional Convention.

~

After they arrived, Washington gave Lee some cash to spend and bought him items including soap, a powder puff, a black silk handkerchief, stockings, and new breeches.

When the convention began, fifty-five delegates were gathered at the Pennsylvania State House, later called Independence Hall. They chose George Washington to act as the president of the convention. To oversee the proceedings, Washington sat in a tall mahogany chair at a desk placed on a raised platform in the front of the room.

The creation of the Constitution of the United States began during the sweltering summer of 1787. Despite the intense heat, the windows of the Assembly Room were closed so that no one could overhear the discussion inside.

As Washington presided over the meeting, William Lee would have been nearby, dressed in his red-and-white livery, waiting in case his master needed him. Washington said little during the convention, and listened carefully as the delegates discussed and debated and argued over the Constitution. One issue caused more division than all the rest: slavery. Some delegates argued passionately against slavery. Others argued passionately for it.

Unlike in the Northern states, the economies of Southern states were based almost entirely on farming, which required many laborers. Most of those laborers were enslaved people. As the fierce arguments continued, it became clear that Southern delegates would not approve the Constitution unless slavery was allowed to continue.

The division between the two sides was so deep there was a real possibility that America would become two nations, divided into Northern and Southern states. In order to create one nation out of thirteen states, the delegates compromised, and the Constitution was worded in such a way as to allow slavery to continue. Although the word "slavery" is not used in the document, indirect references to enslaved people exist in the Constitution. One example is found in Article I, Section 2, which explains that a state's number of representatives in Congress would be "determined by adding to the whole Number of free persons, including those bound to Service for a Term of Years, and excluding Native Americans not taxed, three fifths of all other Persons" (i.e., enslaved black people). This last clause is sometimes known as the Three-Fifths Compromise.

In his notes, James Madison described a comment made by Benjamin Franklin. While presiding over the convention, George Washington sat in a high-backed chair that had half a sun painted at the top. Day after day, as the battle over the Constitution raged and the unity of the nation was in doubt, Franklin looked at the painted sun above Washington's head and wondered whether the sun—like the new nation—was "rising or setting." Once the Constitution was signed, Benjamin Franklin remarked that "at length I have the happiness to know that it is a rising and not a setting Sun."

It took the Declaration of Independence to plant the seeds of freedom in the American colonies. It took the Revolutionary War for the thirteen colonies to break away from England. It took the Constitution to turn thirteen independent states into the United States of America.

But the nation continued to be divided over slavery. Seventy-five years later, long after William Lee and other enslaved people fought for the freedom of the colonies, there would still be no resolution. Only after years of Civil War was slavery abolished, in 1865.

~

Once the Constitution was ratified, William Lee and George Washington returned to Mount Vernon. Lee continued his work as before even though his knee likely still caused him great pain. The next year, 1788, Lee suffered another injury that changed his life. On March 1, Washington wrote in his journal that he "sent my Waiter Will to Alexandria to the Post Office he fell at Mr. Porters door and broke the Pan [kneecap] of his other Knee." William Lee had been Washington's valet for twenty years and was by his side throughout eight years of war. Even so, in his

This is a detail of the "rising sun" chair where George Washington sat while presiding over the 1787 Constitutional Convention.

personal journal Washington describes Lee as "my Waiter Will"—a man who suddenly, at thirty-six years old, could no longer physically accomplish his assigned duties.

Every enslaved person at Mount Vernon was expected to work hard. Lee was no exception. Washington assigned him a task where he could sit down: he learned to make shoes. While Lee was getting used to the changes in his life, a big change was coming for his master. Later that year, George Washington was unanimously elected as the first president of the United States of America.

Washington planned to travel to New York City for his inauguration, and Lee planned to go with him. He had been with his master in New York during the Revolution, and again after the war. He wanted to be with Washington in the city that was now the temporary capital of the United States.

William Lee was willing to travel even though his knee injuries were serious and would make traveling difficult and painful for him. But by the time they reached Philadelphia, Lee had an open wound near his knee and was in no condition to keep riding. On April 19, 1789, Washington's secretary, Tobias Lear, sent a letter about Lee's situation to Clement Biddle, who lived in Philadelphia. He wrote, "Will appears to be in too bad a state to travel at present; I shall therefore leave him—and will be much obliged to you if you will send him on to New York as soon as he can bear the journey without injury. . . . He dresses his knee himself and therefore will stand in no need of a Doctor unless it should grow worse." At the end of the letter, Lear wrote a PS: "Will has just told me that he hopes to be well enough to go on."

But he wasn't. The best doctors available were called in to care for Lee. Biddle checked on him and updated George Washington on April 27, 1789, that Lee "continues too bad to remove—Doctor Smith was uneasy without some other experience'd Surgeon or Physician to look at his knee, and I called on Doctor Hutchinson. They are of opinion that the present Sore reaches to the joint and that it would be very improper to remove him at least for a week or two."

Washington went on to New York City without Lee and was inaugurated on April 30, 1789. The president had a large job ahead of him, but he was concerned about Lee's welfare. Three days after his inauguration, Lear wrote Biddle to say that President Washington "would thank you to propose it to Billy, when he can be removed, to return home again, for he cannot possibly be of any service here, and perhaps will require a person to attend upon him constantly—if he should incline to return to Mt Vernon you will be so kind as to have him sent in the first vessel that sails after he can be removed with safety—but if he is still anxious to come on here the President would gratify him altho' he will be troublesome—He has been an old Servant & a faithful one—this is enough for the President to gratify him in every reasonable wish."

Lee was determined to get to New York. He'd been in Philadelphia under a doctor's care for more than a month when Clement Biddle wrote Lear on May 25, 1789, saying, "I shall have a Steel made this Day by directions of Dr Hutchinson to strengthen Billy's Knee which will not only render his traveling more safe but Enable him in some measure to walk & I shall send him on some Day this Week."

On Wednesday morning, June 15, 1789, William Lee arrived in New York City by ferry. Lee almost certainly remembered the experiences he'd shared with Washington there during the Revolution. Now he was back in the city and his master was the president of the United States. A hired coach took Lee to the president's house at 3 Cherry Street.

Biddle wrote to Lear on June 19, "I hope that Billy got safe to New York without accident." His letter also indicated that the best medical care had been given to Lee while in Philadelphia. Biddle explained to Lear that he was pulling together the bills incurred from Lee's care, and told Lear, "It will be with a heavy expense." To update Biddle, Lear wrote, "Billy arrived here safe & well on Wednesday Morning; he seems not to have lost much flesh by his misfortunes."

Lee may have been impressed with the elegantly furnished house on Cherry Street. Its walls were papered and the floors were covered with expensive carpets. But soon it became clear that with all the activities necessary to the running of the president's house, the Cherry Street residence wasn't big enough. When the French ambassador moved out of a bigger house at 39–41 Broadway, the Washington family moved in.

Washington settled into life as president in New York City. Lee's bad knees likely prevented him from doing much work at the executive mansion, and the cobblestone streets surely made getting around the city

William Lee assisted his master as he sat each morning at this dressing table. Washington shaved himself each day, and then Lee would have dressed and powdered the president's hair. When Washington moved to the house on Broadway, he purchased this piece of French furniture from the previous occupant. He used it for the rest of his life.

This is a re-creation at Mount Vernon of the room where William Lee worked making shoes.

a challenge. Lee stayed in New York about fourteen months before returning home to Mount Vernon in August of 1790.

That fall, Washington and his family prepared to move to Philadelphia, which would be the nation's capital until 1800 when it was moved permanently to Washington, D.C. William Lee did not accompany them there; he stayed behind at Mount Vernon.

~

President Washington ran the nation. But he also ran Mount Vernon from a distance. With William Lee back at Mount Vernon, Washington expected him to be a leader there. In a letter to his farm manager on November 18, 1792, Washington wrote that his people who worked in the Mount Vernon mansion were to be "kept *steadily* to work at that place; under Will, or some other, if he cannot keep them to their business."

Eventually Lee became a full-time cobbler who made shoes for the hundreds of enslaved individuals at Mount Vernon. Washington gave orders that the hides of dead cattle should be tanned and the leather used to repair shoes and for innersoles. In a letter on May 18, 1794, Washington wrote, "Mulatto Will should be kept close to making Shoes, that they may be in readiness by the time they are wanted. He is slow, and sickness, or other interruption may throw this business behind."

Washington may have thought he was slow at his work, but that year Lee produced more than 160 pairs of shoes for the plantation, and repaired many more.

~

When visitors who had been soldiers during the Revolutionary War came to Mount Vernon, Lee wanted to see them. According to George Washington Parke (G.W.P.) Custis, if a veteran arrived, Lee "would send his compliments to the soldier, requesting an interview at his quarters. It was never denied, and Billy, after receiving a warm grasp of the hand, would say, 'Ah, colonel, glad to see you; we of the army don't see one another often in these peaceful times. Glad to see your honor looking so well; remember you at headquarters. The new-time people don't know what we old soldiers did and suffered for the country in the old war. Was it not cold enough at Valley Forge? Yes, was it; and I am sure you remember it was hot enough at Monmouth. Ah, colonel, I am a poor cripple; can't ride now, so I make shoes and think of the old times; the gineral often stops his horse here, to inquire if I want anything. I want for nothing, thank God, but the use of my limbs.'"

Custis said that after the visitors paid their respects to the "retired chief" they gave a tip to the "old body-servant of the Revolution."

House for Families Site

CHAPTER TWO

Christopher Sheels

Christopher Sheels was born into slavery at Mount Vernon in 1775, the same year George Washington was chosen to command the Continental Army. His mother, whose name was Alce (Alice) had at least six children, including Sheels. He is the only one of Alce's children known to have had a last name. Historians think his father may have been a white man named Christopher Shade (sometimes spelled Sheldes), who worked as a wagon driver at Mount Vernon from December of 1770 to July of 1774.

Sheels grew up in the shadow of Washington's mansion. He and his family lived in the nearby slave quarters known as the House for Families. This large communal building was home to those who worked in or around the mansion.

As a small child, Sheels would have spent time in and around the buildings that surrounded Washington's house. He probably played marbles and darted in and out of the Spinners House, one of the buildings on the north lane of Mount Vernon, where his mother worked. Although Sheels' mother, Alce, was assigned duties in the house when needed, she usually worked as a

TOP: As a child Christopher Sheels and his family would have lived in the quarters for enslaved people known as the House for Families. Edward Savage, a popular artist of the day, visited Mount Vernon and painted this view sometime between 1787 and 1792.

BOTTOM: A close-up detail of the House for Families. This building was torn down during the winter of 1792–93. New quarters were built behind the greenhouse.

seamstress who sewed shirts for the people who lived at Mount Vernon. Another of Alce's assignments was running a spinning wheel. Sheels would have grown used to the whirring sound of the wheel as his mother spun sheep's wool into thread. He also would have heard the repeated *clunk clunk, clunk clunk* of the loom as the hired weaver took the wool thread made by his mother and wove it into fabric.

Sheels' grandmother Doll, often called Old Doll, was the cook. She prepared food for the Washington family in the kitchen, a building set apart from the main house. All year long, Sheels likely smelled the wood fire in the hearth while watching his grandmother cook. On cold winter days the kitchen would have been toasty warm. In the summer, the constant cooking fire would have felt like an inferno.

Christopher Sheels' family had lived and worked at Mount Vernon since Martha Custis married George Washington in 1759. His grandmother Doll was one of the enslaved women the new bride brought with her when she moved to the plantation from New Kent County, in southern Virginia

Christopher Sheels likely spent a lot of time in this spinning room with his mother, Alce. She worked at a spinning wheel like the one on the right, making thread or yarn used to make clothing. The large piece of equipment on the left is a loom for weaving fabric.

near Williamsburg. As Christopher Sheels was growing up, he probably saw Martha Washington often. Every morning the mistress of Mount Vernon would discuss the day's meals with his grandmother.

But Sheels could not have known the impact Washington's past—the life she led before she moved to Mount Vernon—would have on his own future.

Martha Washington had been married before she became the wife of George Washington. Her first husband, Daniel Parke Custis, was probably the wealthiest man in Virginia. He owned thousands of acres of land and about three hundred people. They had two small children together when Custis died unexpectedly at a young age. He did not leave a will detailing what would happen to his property at his death, and so his estate was divided up according to the inheritance laws of Virginia. This meant that two thirds of his property would be split between his children. One third of his property would be his wife's dower (widow's) share. During her lifetime, Martha Custis had the use of one third of her late husband's estate that included personal possessions such as furniture, land, and enslaved people. The men, women, and children who were counted in her lifetime widow's share are sometimes called "dower slaves."

The law allowed Martha Custis to benefit from her dower inheritance as long as she was alive. But she could not sell any of it—not the land and not the enslaved people. When Martha Custis died, everything would be divided among her living Custis descendants.

Christopher Sheels was part of the dower estate of Martha Custis. So were his siblings, his mother Alce, his aunts, his uncles, and his grandmother Doll. Therefore, Sheels' life would always be bound by the terms of Martha Washington's inherited estate.

At Mount Vernon, with some exceptions, each enslaved African American belonged to either George Washington or to Martha Washington's dower estate. But because the two groups lived together as one community and intermarried, that meant that for some families, the husband belonged to George Washington while the wife and children belonged to Martha Custis Washington's dower estate. For others, the opposite held true.

Christopher Sheels was related to both groups of people. His aunt Lucy (his mother's sister) was married to Frank Lee (William Lee's brother). George Washington owned William and Frank Lee. Although every enslaved person at Mount Vernon knew who owned him or her, in day-to-day life it didn't seem to matter, because George Washington was the master of everyone.

While Sheels and the other enslaved children at the plantation were small, they were given tasks such as fetching wood or drawing and hauling water from the well. The work required of them increased as they grew up. When Christopher Sheels was still a child he was assigned to work with one of the carpenters. By the age of twelve he was issued a hoe, and went to work in the fields full-time.

The next year Sheels' responsibilities would change drastically. That was the year William Lee broke his second kneecap and was no longer physically able to work as Washington's valet. Perhaps William Lee told his master that Sheels, his brother's nephew, could step in.

In 1788, thirteen-year-old Christopher Sheels replaced William Lee as Washington's personal valet.

~

Working in the mansion house rather than the field meant visitors would see young Sheels, so he wore the same type of livery as William Lee had before him. But being Washington's personal servant was not easy, even if the clothing was nicer and the tasks less physical than carpentry or laboring in the fields. Sheels' workday began long before his master woke each morning at five o'clock, and ended long after he went to bed. Working in the Washingtons' house was also a double-edged sword in the sense that the people who served the Washington family in their home, like Sheels, were constantly supervised. Someone saw everything they did and heard everything they said. Although field workers were supervised, they were not watched every moment, which gave them a little bit of space to talk and be themselves.

In 1789, the year after Sheels became a valet, George Washington was elected president. When Washington left Mount Vernon for New York City, the first capital of the United States, Christopher Sheels went with him.

Jubilant crowds of people gathered to greet his master in each city they traveled through. Fourteen-year-old Sheels saw firsthand how famous his master was, and he may well have been stunned by the cities he saw along the way to New York. The only city Sheels had likely ever seen before was Alexandria, Virginia.

On their way to Washington's inauguration they stopped in Philadelphia, where it became clear that William Lee was not physically able to continue on to New York City. Sheels said goodbye to Lee as they left him behind to get medical treatment for his knee.

April 30, 1789, was President Washington's inauguration day. As Washington's valet, Sheels likely got his clothes ready that morning: a snow-white shirt with wide pleated ruffles made of the finest linen, a dark brown broadcloth coat with gleaming gold buttons engraved with eagles, a matching waistcoat and knee breeches, white stockings, black shoes with buckles, and a dress sword. Since Washington never wore a wig, it may have been Sheels who, to prepare for this formal occasion, brushed Washington's hair back, fastened it, puffed white powder onto it, and tucked the ends neatly into a black silk hair bag.

When Washington dressed that day he understood the public would watch his every move. Everything he did, everything he said, and even the clothes he wore would be noticed. Sheels would have helped him into his dark brown suit made of broadcloth manufactured in America, rather than cloth from England or France. Even at his inauguration, Sheels' master was making a silent statement that America would soon be producing its own high-quality goods.

Now that the Washington family lived in New York, Sheels needed more new clothes. His master ordered him a new hat, shirt, shoes, and several pairs of stockings to wear with his knee breeches.

~

Christopher Sheels lived in New York City for about a year while serving as valet for President Washington. Then in 1790, Congress made a decision that would require

The figure dressed in livery on the far right could represent either Christopher Sheels or William Lee. The family posed for artist Edward Savage in New York during the winter of 1789–90 for this painting, titled *The Washington Family*.

Sheels to make another big move. It was agreed that New York City would not remain the nation's capital. A permanent capital city would be built in an area more centrally located between the Northern and Southern states. Washington decided the new federal city (Washington, District of Columbia) would be built on the banks of the Potomac River a few miles upriver from Mount Vernon. Construction of the city would take about ten years. In the meantime, the capital would relocate from New York City to Philadelphia, Pennsylvania—meaning Washington and his household would go there too.

Sheels returned to Mount Vernon with Washington for a few months between moves. By November 21, 1790, he was on his way to the president's house in Philadelphia. In addition to Sheels, the Washingtons planned to take several other enslaved people with them, including Austin, Moll, Giles, Oney Judge, Hercules, and Richmond.

Hercules was Washington's cook and Richmond was Hercules' son. In a letter to Tobias Lear on November 22, 1790, Washington wrote, "Richmond and Christopher [Sheels] embarked [to Philadelphia] yesterday by Water."

~

Those left behind at Mount Vernon were concerned about the safe travel of Sheels, now about fifteen years old, and Richmond, about thirteen, by ship. In a letter to his uncle, George Augustine Washington wrote from Mount Vernon on December 28, 1790, that he was "pleased to find by the former that the apprehensions for the safety of Christopher and Richmond are removed."

Sheels settled into life in Philadelphia at the president's house. He wore new stockings and shoes, and ruffled shirts. On George Washington's birthday, Martha Washington gave Sheels a half dollar to spend on presents for his family back home.

In the spring of 1791, Christopher Sheels stayed behind in Philadelphia when Washington left for a tour of the Southern states that would take nearly three months to complete. Sheels was likely working in the house on April 5 when Edmund Randolph, a familiar visitor, arrived at the door of the president's residence on Market Street.

The Washington and Randolph families were both from Virginia and had been friends for many years. Randolph was serving in Washington's Cabinet as the United States attorney general. Knowing the president was not at home, Randolph asked to visit with Lady Washington. He was not there for a social call. He had information he wanted the Washingtons to know.

Randolph told Martha Washington that the very next day, three of the people he owned would be claiming their freedom under a law called the Act for the Gradual Abolition of Slavery. This Pennsylvania law, passed in 1780 near the end of the Revolutionary War, was created to slowly abolish slavery. Eight years later, an amendment was added that allowed any enslaved man or woman to apply for freedom if they had lived in the state continuously for six months. Even though the Constitution allowed slavery to exist nationally, it was possible for this law to pass in Pennsylvania because each state retained the right to enact its own laws to govern itself.

Randolph warned Lady Washington that her own family's enslaved people might also try to claim their freedom through the Gradual Abolition Act. The Washingtons had been living in Philadelphia for nearly six months—and Martha Washington had no intention of letting that happen.

The same day as Randolph's visit, Tobias Lear wrote the president to explain the situation. Lear asked George Washington "to give directions in the matter respecting the blacks in this family."

The president replied on April 12, 1791:

"I know not, and therefore beg you will take the best advise you can on the subject, and in case it shall be found that any of my Slaves may, or any for them shall attempt their freedom at the expiration of six months, it is my wish and desire that you would send the whole, or such part of them as Mrs. Washington may not chuse to keep, home—for although I do not think they would be benefitted by the change, yet the idea of freedom might be too great a temptation for them to resist. At any rate it might, if they conceived they had a right to it, make them insolent in a State of Slavery. As all except Hercules and Paris are dower negroes, it behoves me to prevent the emancipation of them, otherwise I shall not only loose the use of them, but may have them to pay for. If upon taking good advise it is found expedient to send them back to Virginia, I wish to have it accomplished under pretext that may deceive both them and the Public;—and none I think would so effectually do this, as Mrs. Washington coming to Virginia next month (towards the middle or latter end of it, as she seemed to have a wish to do) if she can accomplish it by any convenient and agreeable means, with the assistance of the Stage Horses &c. This would naturally bring her maid and Austin—and Hercules under the idea of coming home to Cook whilst we remained there, might be sent on in the Stage. Whether there is occasion for this or not according to the result of your enquiries, or issue the thing as it may, I request that these Sentiments and this advise may be known to none but yourself & Mrs. Washington."

President Washington determined he would actively prevent the men and women whom he and his wife's dower estate owned from gaining their freedom. To do that, he needed to ensure that none of them would be able to claim residence for six continuous months in Pennsylvania—and he hoped to accomplish this in a way that would hide his true motives from the enslaved community and the public.

As the president's letter to Lear notes, the majority of the enslaved people the Washingtons had taken with them to Philadelphia were part of Martha Washington's dower estate. This presented a financial concern for George Washington. Even though he was the president of the United States and owned a lot of property, he didn't have much cash. Like all husbands then, Washington managed his wife's business affairs. He realized that if any of the African Americans in whom she had a life interest claimed their freedom, he would be required to pay back their value to the Custis estate, and might even be sued by the Custis heirs. He hoped to avoid this.

The Pennsylvania Society for Promoting the Abolition of Slavery was an active group in the city. Since Philadelphia was the nation's capital, there were many members of Congress living there who were slave owners. In order to avoid a clash with these slave-owning federal officials, the abolitionists agreed to "give no advice and take no measures for liberating those Slaves that belonged to governmental officials."

But Lear wrote to Washington that even without the influence of the abolition society, there were those in the city who would give advice to enslaved people and would "use all means to entice them from their masters."

Randolph suggested a loophole that the Washingtons could use to get around the Gradual Abolition of Slavery Act. If an enslaved person went out of the state of Pennsylvania for even one day, when they returned, the clock on their their six months of residency started all over again.

Time was running out if the Washingtons wanted to take advantage of this loophole. By the end of May, some of the people they enslaved would have lived continuously for six months in Pennsylvania. The Washingtons had just one month to get each of them out of the state for at least one day; otherwise they could claim their freedom.

For some of the members of their household, the six-month residency date was farther off. At the time, Austin, the footman, had gone home to Mount Vernon to visit his wife. Lear wrote that "this will oblige him to commence a new date for six month from his return—which will be next week." One of the others, Richmond, the son of Hercules the cook, was already set to leave "in a Vessel that sails tomorrow for Alexandria." As to Richmond's father, Lear received word from Washington that perhaps Hercules could be persuaded to return to Mount Vernon for a visit earlier than planned.

The matter of the teenagers, Christopher Sheels and Oney Judge, Martha Washington's personal maid, would be settled by Lady Washington, who planned to take them with her on a short trip out of state. She arranged to visit her friends Senator Philemon Dickinson and his wife, Mary, who lived about thirty miles away in Trenton, New Jersey. Lear wrote Washington that this would "carry them out of the State; so that in this way I think the matter may be managed very well."

As a faithful friend and employee of the Washington family, Tobias Lear helped them ensure that they could prevent their enslaved people from gaining freedom through the Gradual Abolition of Slavery Act. Yet personally, Lear was uncomfortable about the deception. In the same letter he wrote his boss, "You will permit me now, Sir, (and I am sure you will pardon me for doing it) to declare, that no consideration should induce me to take these steps to prolong the slavery of a human being, had I not the fullest confidence that they will at some future period be liberated, and the strongest conviction that their situation with you is far preferable to what they would probably obtain in a state of freedom."

This 1791 letter indicates that Lear believed Washington's enslaved people would eventually be freed. It also shows that Lear thought they were better off being part of Washington's household than they would be if they were emancipated and facing the challenges of living as free blacks. In their letters to each other, neither Washington nor Lear considered what the enslaved people wanted for themselves.

It is unknown how much the enslaved men and women in the presidential household knew about the Gradual Abolition Act. But if the people Randolph owned were aware of it, it is highly likely that the people George and Martha Washinton owned were too. If so, were they counting down the days until they had lived in Pennsylvania for six months? Were they allowing themselves to dream about being free? Were they wrestling with the realization that if they were free, they would probably never again see their families at Mount Vernon? Were they wondering what sort of paying job they could get? Were they wondering where they would live once they were on their own?

If Sheels and Judge were aware of the six-month residency, their hope for a chance at freedom would have died the moment they found out that they would be traveling to the Dickinson household in New Jersey with their mistress. On May 15, 1791, Lear confirmed in a letter to Washington, "On Tuesday Mrs. Washington proposes going over to Jersey for a few days." He added, "Mrs. Washington takes the children with her & Christopher & Oney."

Martha Washington's deceitful plan to visit New Jersey, couched as an innocent outing to visit friends, was successful. None of the men and women who served the Washingtons in Philadelphia ever gained their freedom through the Gradual Abolition Act. The president and his wife made sure of it.

~

During his years as president, Washington and his family occasionally went home to Mount Vernon to stay for a couple of months at a time. In September 1791, Christopher Sheels and the other enslaved people the Washingtons took to Philadelphia with them returned to Virginia.

At that point, Sheels had been serving as personal valet to the president of the United States of America for more than two years. He'd lived in the presidential homes in New York City and Philadelphia. He'd witnessed the birth of a new government. He'd watched his master establish a new form of leadership for that government. He'd heard—and served—the Founding Fathers and Mothers of the new nation.

But when the president and his family returned to Philadelphia after their stay at home, sixteen-year-old Sheels was left behind at Mount Vernon. It will never be known how he felt when the Washingtons' carriages rolled away without him. He would never again return to the capital city. Since Washington was no longer residing at Mount Vernon, Christopher Sheels was put back to work as a carpenter.

Although Sheels may have been out of Washington's sight, Washington still kept tabs on him, as he did everyone else at Mount Vernon. Since Washington couldn't witness the work happening on his eight-thousand-acre plantation for himself, he established a system that would allow him to supervise from a distance. On each of his five farms he chose an overseer. On three of his farms, Washington placed enslaved men as overseers: Davy at River Farm, Morris at Dogue Run Farm, and Will at Muddy Hole Farm. Every week the overseer of each farm reported to the farm manager details of exactly what work was done and by whom. It is unknown whether Davy, Morris, and Will had been taught to read and write and turned in a written report, or whether they gave their report orally. After gathering these reports, the farm manager, who supervised the entire plantation, wrote long letters to Washington describing everything that happened that week. In return, Washington wrote long letters of instructions to his farm manager.

Washington finished his first term as president and was reelected to a second term. During those years, the weekly farm reports mention Sheels working at a variety of tasks, including making planks, making shingles, laying shingles, driving a wagon, hauling timber, working in the brickyard, building a shed, and sawing wood.

When Washington's second term was over in 1797, the exhausted former president and his family prepared to leave Philadelphia. Moving home for good, they packed up the presidential household, including their pets. Washington wrote Tobias Lear, "On one side I am called upon to remember the Parrot, on the other to remember the dog. For my own part I should not pine much if both were forgot."

Once Washington had returned to Mount Vernon, Sheels again worked as his personal valet, in addition to other responsibilities around the house, such as serving meals when guests dined at Mount Vernon.

In October of that year, a dog bit Sheels on his finger. It may have been the same dog Washington mentioned in his letter to Lear, which belonged to Martha Washington's granddaughter, Eleanor Parke (Nelly) Custis. Sheels' dog bite was a bad one, and the situation was all the more serious because the dog was "supposed to be a little diseased."

As a slave owner, George Washington was harsh if he suspected someone was pretending to be ill to get out of working. But when his enslaved people were truly sick or injured, Washington did what was necessary to provide medical treatment. After Sheels was bitten, Washington sent for Dr. Craik, who "cut out so far as He could, the place Bit—applyed Ointment to keep it open. And put the Boy under a Course of mercury."

A few days later the dog died "in a state of Madness [rabies]." Washington was concerned for Sheels. He'd heard about a man named William Stoy in Lebanon, Pennsylvania, who was thought to have a cure for

Christopher Sheels probably lived in the enslaved men's quarters behind the greenhouse. This is a reconstruction at Mount Vernon that shows how it may have looked.

people bitten by rabid animals. Washington planned to send Sheels to be treated by Stoy.

Washington gave Sheels $25 to pay his travel expenses. He sent with him a letter to give to Stoy that put the young man "under Your care, Trusting You will do every thing in Your Power, to prevent any bad consequences from the Bite, And have at the same time wrote to Mr Slough in Lancaster to pay whatever is Your charge. And whenever the Boy arrives do write me, And your Opinion of Him—for besides the call of Humanity, I am particularly anxious for His cure, He being my own Body servant."

Five days later, Stoy wrote to Washington to say that Sheels is "in no danger of the account of that bite, Since he hath taken my medicin . . . rest assured Sheels is Safe."

Twenty-two-year-old Sheels had traveled alone to Pennsylvania for medical care. Once he was treated and was out of danger, he could have run away. He could have left his mother, grandmother, aunts, uncles, and cousins back at Mount Vernon and escaped. He had the money. He had the opportunity.

But he didn't. Sheels returned to his family—and to slavery. When he got back to Mount Vernon, Sheels returned $12—his unspent travel expenses—to his owner, George Washington.

~

About two years later, during the summer of 1799, twenty-four-year-old Christopher Sheels fell in love. The young woman, whose name is unknown, was owned by Roger West and lived at West Grove Plantation, located a few miles north of Mount Vernon.

At Mount Vernon, enslaved people worked six days a week and had Sunday off. But those who worked in the mansion, like Sheels, almost certainly varied their days off, because even on Sundays the Washington family still required their dinner to be cooked and served, their rooms cleaned, and their chamber pots emptied.

In their small amount of free time, the enslaved people tended their own gardens, raised their own chickens, hunted game for their tables, cut firewood, washed clothes, cooked food, and visited with family and friends. On Saturday nights, it was not unusual for those who lived on different plantations to visit each other. Maybe that is how Sheels met the woman he loved.

Sheels needed to ask Washington's permission to marry her, since she belonged to Roger West. Washington had no objection if West gave his permission too.

Marriages between enslaved people were not legal in the eyes of the law. However, their marriages were recognized within their own communities, and at Mount Vernon they were recognized by George Washington. In lists of his workers, he noted the names of spouses, and he allowed spouses who lived on his farms or nearby plantations to visit each other. After Christopher Sheels was married, he was permitted to travel to West Grove Plantation and would have visited his wife as often as possible.

In September 1799, Washington had what was for him an unpleasant surprise. Someone found a handwritten note in the yard at Mount Vernon and handed it over to him. While no one knows where the note came from, it contained a plan for Christopher Sheels and his wife to run away. Washington immediately wrote Roger West to let him know what he had discovered. He suggested that since West was closer to Alexandria, he would be better able to make "discovery of the Vessel, they contemplate to escape in."

Washington wrote that he believed Roger West "would be equally desirous to arrest their project; but if, as some say, she is free;

According to Virginia law, an enslaved person needed a pass or letter any time they traveled away from their own home. This is an example of a travel permit, although it is not one from George Washington. On October 29, 1771, two enslaved people, Bobb and George, had permission to travel about one hundred miles from Fredericksburg, Virginia, to James Mercer at Williamsburg.

Permit

Negro Bobb. Coachman & Negro George. Postillion.
Without molestation.
To Pass. from Fredericksburg. in Spots on to James
Mercer Esqr at Williamsburg. with a Coach and Six Horses.
Commited to there care.
The severel inn Keepers whare they may have occation to
Bate. are requested to furnish them with what may be
Needfull. for the Horses & them selves. agreeable to the usual.
Custom of victualling of Negros on suchlike Emargencies
Taking care to sett down the Expence on the back of this
Passport. with the Innkeepers Name. that Mr. Mercer may
Discharge the same on his return.

Thos. Oliver

Steward to Jas Mercer Esqr

To all Concearnd

N.B. they begin there Jurney on the 29th Octr 1771

and as others, that you are about to make her so, our cases differ." Washington understood the difference in their circumstances. West could free Sheels' wife, or might have already freed her. Washington could not free Sheels because Sheels was enslaved by Martha Washington's dower estate. Whenever she died, Sheels would go to one of her heirs. If Roger West answered George Washington's letter, his response does not survive today.

Washington likely confronted Sheels about his plans to escape, though no documentary evidence exists that indicates whether or not Sheels was disciplined. Today, we can only imagine the devastation Sheels must have felt when he realized the escape he planned with his wife had failed.

His chance at freedom was gone.

CHAPTER THREE

Caroline (Branham) & Peter Hardiman

Caroline was an African American woman who was one of the enslaved people in Martha Washington's dower estate. She worked as a housemaid in the mansion, and likely had a daily routine. Long before dawn, Caroline would have left her bed in her quarters and made her way toward the house in the dark. At the door, Caroline would have wiped her feet to make sure she didn't track in any dirt. She would have walked quietly so as not to wake the family or guests.

During winter, Caroline must have shivered in the cold as she placed the wood in the fireplace. She lit a fire in each room to knock the chill off before the Washington family got out of bed.

With the fires beginning to crackle, she cleaned the hearths and mantels. In the parlors and dining room, Caroline wiped the frames of the paintings, shook dust from the curtains, and swept the floors. In the central passageway, Caroline dusted the glass case that held the key to the Bastille as well as the framed drawing of the French political prison in ruins. Both were gifts from the Marquis de Lafayette, the French general of the American Revolution, who was like a son to Washington.

When she cleaned the staircase she controlled the dust by throwing wet sand on the top stair and sweeping it down step by step. Caroline dusted the polished walnut railing that turned the corner to the second story.

By the time those tasks were completed, the family and overnight guests would be getting

One of Caroline's duties as housemaid each morning was to empty chamber pots like the one shown here, which were used during the night by the Washington family and their guests. (This particular porcelain chamber pot did not belong to the Washingtons but to their friends, the family of Samuel Powel, who lived in Philadelphia.)

up. Once they left their rooms Caroline took the sheets off their beds, shook the feather mattresses, turned them, and put the sheets back on. She brushed dust from the bed curtains and cleaned under the beds. She emptied and cleaned the chamber pots that had been used during the night. Then Caroline poured a little bit of water into the pots to cut down on the smell and mess for the next time she emptied them.

~

Caroline's husband, Peter Hardiman, belonged to Martha Washington's son, Jacky Custis. Jacky was four when his father, Daniel Parke Custis, died in 1757. Jacky's sister, Martha Parke (Patcy) Custis, was about two. Once the siblings' mother married George Washington, their stepfather managed her business affairs—and theirs.

Patcy Custis died when she was a teenager, so her share of the Custis estate was divided between her mother and her brother, Jacky. As soon as Jacky was an adult he took possession of his very large inheritance. Peter Hardiman was part of the group of people Jacky inherited when he came of age.

In 1774, not long after his sister Patcy's death, Jacky Custis married a woman named Eleanor Calvert. The couple bought a plantation near Alexandria called Abingdon. Soon their family grew to include three daughters and a son.

In 1781 Jacky Custis died suddenly, leaving his widow, Eleanor, with their four small children. Like his father before him, Jacky Custis died without a will. Eleanor Custis, like Martha Washington before her, had the use and benefit of one third of her deceased husband's property during her lifetime. Peter Hardiman belonged to the estate of Jacky Custis.

Eleanor Custis maintained close ties with Martha and George Washington after Jacky's death. They often visited each other, and since Peter Hardiman worked with the carriage horses, he traveled with Eleanor Custis and her children from Abingdon whenever they visited Mount Vernon.

Peter Hardiman and Caroline, who lived at Mount Vernon, met, fell in love, and were married. But like many other couples who lived on different plantations, Hardiman and Caroline spent a lot of time apart. Each of them must have looked forward to Eleanor Custis' visits with the Washingtons so they could be together.

In 1783, Caroline was nearing the birth of her first child at Mount Vernon. On September 3 of that year, far away in Paris, France, Benjamin Franklin, John Adams, and two other American officials signed the Treaty of Paris. This document brought an official end to the American Revolution after eight long and difficult years of war.

Even if Caroline had known about the signing of the peace treaty, it would not have made any difference in her life. It didn't free her or the child she was carrying. The only effect the treaty had on Caroline was that it meant her master, General George Washington, was coming home.

When Caroline's baby was born two months later, on November 6, the child did not survive.

That same year, 1783, Eleanor Custis remarried. After her marriage to Dr. David Stuart, her two oldest two daughters, Elizabeth Parke (Betsy) Custis and Martha Parke (Patty) Custis, stayed with her and her new husband. She allowed her two youngest children, George Washington Parke (called Wash or Washington) Custis and Eleanor Parke (Nelly) Custis, to live with their grandmother and stepgrandfather at Mount Vernon. When Washington and William Lee returned from the war on Christmas Eve, Washington got reacquainted with his step-grandchildren.

After being away from Mount Vernon for eight years commanding the Continental Army, Washington recognized that his home and farm needed lots of attention. Ultimately, he wanted his plantation to be as self-sufficient as possible. He didn't want to buy anything that could be produced by his own enslaved people at Mount Vernon. If a specific skill was needed that no one on the plantation possessed, Washington rented an enslaved person from another plantation owner or hired an indentured worker to accomplish the task. Eventually the people Washington owned, rented, indentured, or hired allowed his plantation to be nearly self-sufficient. The people laboring there produced tanned leather for shoes, made iron tools in the blacksmith shop, and milled corn and wheat. Washington owned carpenters, coopers who made buckets and barrels, brick makers and bricklayers, spinners, weavers, and seamstresses.

Another way Mount Vernon was able to be self-sufficient was thanks to the annual fish harvest. Each April and May, shad and herring swam up the Potomac River. When the fish were running, most of the other work on the plantation stopped so that the workforce could concentrate their labor on processing the catch. Everyone was reassigned to work the fish harvest, including Caroline and the others who normally worked in the mansion. Once the catch was pulled from the river, each fish was gutted and the head removed. Nothing was wasted at Mount Vernon, so the fish heads and guts were piled onto wagons and taken to the crop fields where they were incorporated into the soil as fertilizer.

As Washington continued to assess the needs of the plantation, he found that no one at Mount Vernon was experienced in horse breeding and handling. But Peter Hardiman, who lived and worked at Abingdon, was. So Washington rented Caroline's husband from his owner, Eleanor Custis Stuart, for one year for the price of £12 . Peter Hardiman came to live at Mount Vernon with his wife.

On March 18, 1785, Caroline and her husband welcomed a son into the world. They named him Wilson. Like other new mothers, Caroline was issued her yearly blanket when her child was born. Like every other child born into slavery, Caroline and Peter Hardiman's son didn't really belong to them. Wilson belonged to the dower estate of Martha Custis Washington because that estate owned his mother, Caroline.

~

Peter Hardiman took care of Washington's horses, stable, and carriages. When the horses were sick or injured, Hardiman decided what to do for them. He took special care of Washington's two purebred racehorses, Leonidas and an Arabian stallion named Magnolia. Hardiman's skill with horses must have been known in the community, because in the fall of 1785 Washington loaned him to his friend William Fitzhugh for a horse race. Fitzhugh wrote Washington a thank-you letter that said, "Thanks for the Loan of Peter—and I am happy that I have it in my Power to send him Home unhurt." Fitzhugh's comment that Hardiman was unhurt might indicate Hardiman was the jockey in the race. If so, he must have ridden the horse to victory, because Fitzhugh added, "Tarquin has recover'd the Laurells he lost at Alexandria."

That same year, Peter Hardiman's responsibilities increased. His master, who constantly sought out more effective methods to improve his crops and equipment, had learned that mules made excellent farm animals. In order to breed mules at Mount Vernon, Washington needed some fine male donkeys. At the time there were very few good donkeys in America. The best in the world were considered to be a large breed in Spain, but it was illegal to export them. Then, in 1785, King Charles III of Spain sent two of his best donkeys as a gift to George Washington. One of them died on the voyage, but the other survived and was named

Edward Savage painted this view of Mount Vernon sometime between 1787 and 1792. The Washington family is shown on the front lawn and enslaved people are in the background. On the right side of the painting is a carriage that would have been under the care of Peter Hardiman.

Royal Gift. About a year later, the Marquis de Lafayette sent Washington a donkey from the island of Malta, whose name was Knight of Malta.

Peter Hardiman supervised a breeding operation using these two donkeys that would not only produce mules for use at Mount Vernon, but would also give his master an opportunity to make extra money. Neighbors paid Washington to have their female horses bred with one of his donkeys.

Washington was known as one of the first large-scale breeders and promoters of mules in America—but it was Peter Hardiman who actually ran the breeding operation.

~

Around Christmastime of 1786, the twelve months that Hardiman had been rented to Washington ended. Washington wrote Eleanor's husband, David Stuart, on February 12, 1787, to say that although Hardiman was helpful at breeding time and when the mares gave birth, others could handle things during the rest of the year. Washington wrote, "I have no desire to keep him, if you find a use for him." But Stuart answered that Hardiman should stay at Mount Vernon for the rest of the year to manage Washington's horse breeding operation.

That year, Caroline and Peter Hardiman welcomed a daughter named Rachel into their family. Another year went by and Washington's agreement was up again. In the meantime, Hardiman told Washington that he wanted to stay at Mount Vernon with his family.

In a letter to David Stuart on January 22, 1788, Washington wrote, "As you have no immediate occasion for Peter in the only line in which he will be useful to you, I shall be very glad to keep him, as well on acct of my Jacks, Stud Horses, Mares, etc., as because he seems unwilling to part with his wife and Children."

The next year, 1789, Caroline gave birth to another daughter, Jemima. It was the same year George Washington was inaugurated as president of the United States. For the next eight years the Washington family would be away from Mount Vernon except for visits. But life there continued for Caroline, Hardiman, and their children, and the couple added another daughter, Leanthe, to their family in 1791.

Two years later, in early 1793, Caroline fell ill for six days. On January 16 the farm manager, Anthony Whitting, wrote to Washington that "Caroline is very unwell has had a Smart fever all last week." Seeing that she suffered with a high fever, Whitting used the typical treatment of the day, bloodletting (opening a vein to let some blood out of the body). He reported that he "bled her in the early part of the week She complaind of a pain in her head & side She is now something better but has a very dry bad Cough I have Given her something to take for it & hope She will Get better." Caroline recovered.

That same year, Caroline and Hardiman had another daughter, named Polly. Two years later, in 1795, another son, Peter, was born. Like other women with young children, Caroline probably cared for her own little ones while doing tasks that would allow her to watch them—such as sewing or spinning thread and yarn. When she was required to do work that prevented her from caring for them, older children or the elderly likely looked after them.

While they were young, Caroline and Peter Hardiman's children would play around the mansion house yard and gardens. In 1790, the farm manager wrote Washington and mentioned that the children of Caroline and Charlotte (also a housemaid and seamstress) "being in the yard certainly made it more difficult to keep it clean." Three years later, Washington complained to his manager that there were "a great number of Negro children at the Quarters belonging to the house people" that were forbidden to go within the enclosed areas of the yard and gardens so they wouldn't be "breaking the shrubs, and doing other mischief."

When Caroline and Peter Hardiman's children reached about twelve years of age they were considered "working boys and girls" and were assigned duties. Their son Wilson, for instance, started working with his father in the stable.

Every so often, Hardiman was able to profit from his talent with horses. Men in the community sometimes paid him for his services as a groom. In fact, any of the enslaved people at Mount Vernon were permitted to make extra money as long as it didn't interfere with their regular work. Caroline sold ducks, chickens, and eggs to George Washington's household. Some people sold brooms, poultry, wild game, honey, and other products on Sundays at Market Square in Alexandria. Those who did needed a pass from their master giving them permission to do business at the market, and they could only do so until 9:00 a.m.—then they had to leave. Selling at the Sunday market meant a very early morning. The nine-mile trip from Mount Vernon to Alexandria by horseback took an hour and a half to two hours each way.

~

George Washington expected a full day of work from himself and everyone else on his plantation, whether they were white farm managers, white hired workers, white indentured workers, or black enslaved workers. Washington would not tolerate idleness in anyone. This expectation was partly due to his exacting personality. But he also needed his workforce to be productive because money was always tight.

Although Washington owned thousands of acres of land, he didn't have much cash. Part of the reason he was cash-poor was that he refused to take a salary during the Revolutionary War. When the Continental Congress unanimously voted him commander in chief of the American army on June 16, 1775, Washington accepted the job, but told Congress that because no amount of money "could have tempted me to have accepted this arduous employment, at the expence of my domestic ease and happiness, I do not wish to make any profit from it."

Instead of being paid for his efforts, Washington simply requested that any money he spent on wartime expenses be paid back to him when the conflict was over. Throughout the war he carefully documented his expenditures for reimbursement.

During eight years of war, Washington served his country for love, not money. But while he was away from home, Mount Vernon didn't prosper financially either. Washington's cash woes worsened upon his return, because the plantation needed improvements. Also a constant parade of guests arrived at his doorstep needing to be fed. Both required money.

Despite their cash shortage, George and

Martha Washington continued to give money to charities and to destitute individuals who came to them for help. Many of the people to whom Washington had loaned money over the years never paid him back. John Mercer was one of them. Washington had been home from the war for about six months when he wrote Mercer on July 8, 1784, saying, "I can only repeat to you, how convenient it would be to me to receive that balance—I do assure you Sir, that I am distressed for want of money."

Strapped as he was, Washington did have an option for raising cash quickly and easily: he could have sold some of the people he owned. But at this point in his life, he would not consider it.

That was not always Washington's position. During the early years of the Revolution, it appears Washington discussed with his farm manager, Lund Washington, the idea of selling some of his enslaved men and women. In a letter on March 11, 1778, Lund Washington wrote to George Washington, "If I can sell the Negroes I mention'd to you by private Sale I will—but the Best way of Sellg is at Publick Sale."

Some letters on this subject between Washington and his farm manager have never been found, and without them it is impossible to know exactly what Washington was thinking. However, Lund Washington's response to one of the missing letters written by George Washington seems to indicate that Washington did not want to sell any of his enslaved people unless they agreed to it. On April 8, the farm manager wrote, "With regard to Sellg the Negroes Mention'd, you have put it out of my power, by saying you woud not sell them without their Consent—I was very near Sellg Bett, indeed I had sold her for £200 to a man liveg in Bottetourt Cty, But her Mother appeard to be so uneasy about it, and Bett herself made such promises of amendment, that I coud not Force her to go with the Man, to another Man at the same time I offed Phillis for £200, but she was so alrmd at the thoughts of being sold that the man cou'd not get her to utter a Word of English, therefore he believed she cou'd not speak—the man was to come two days after—when he came she was Sick & has been ever Since, so that I sold neither of them . . . unless I was to make a Publick Sale of those Negroes & pay no regard to their being Willing or not, I see no probability of sellg them—but this is a matter that may be fixd when I see you, I believe the price of them will keep up at least for this Summer."

Bett and her mother were not purchased that spring, but there is evidence that these two women and seven others were eventually sold. On January 18, 1779, an entry in the farm manager's ledger notes that he received £2,303.19 "Cash for the Following Negroes. Abram, Orford, Tom, Jack, Ede, Fattimore, Phillis, Bett & Jenny." It will likely never be known whether Bett and Phillis consented to be sold away from Mount Vernon.

By the end of the Revolutionary War, several years after these people were sold, Washington's views on slavery had begun to shift. He eventually resolved that he would not buy or sell any more enslaved people, or separate their families. Washington also expressed a desire for legislation that would abolish slavery.

In 1786, two years after Washington asked John Mercer to pay back the money he was owed, Mercer still had not paid in cash. Instead, Mercer offered to repay some of the debt in human beings. Washington wasn't interested. At this point, there were about 216 enslaved people living at Mount Vernon, including the people Washington owned himself and those owned by Martha Washington's dower estate. Washington wrote to John Mercer on September 9, 1786, "I never mean (unless some particular circumstances should compel me to it) to possess another slave by purchase; it being among my first wishes to see some plan adopted, by the legislature by which slavery in this Country may be abolished by slow, sure, & imperceptable degrees."

Mercer continued to try to settle his debt to Washington by turning his enslaved people over to him, but Washington wrote Mercer again on November 24, 1786, "With respect to the negroes, I conclude it is not in my power to answer your wishes—because it is as much against my own inclination as it can be against your's, to hurt the feelings of those unhappy people by a separation of man and wife, or of families."

That same year, Washington's old friend Lafayette informed him that he had bought a plantation in Cayenne, French Guiana. He would emancipate the enslaved people who lived there, and allow them to rent a part of the plantation as free men. On May 10, 1786, Washington wrote Lafayette that his plan was "a generous and noble proof" of his friend's humanity. Then Washington wrote, "Would to God a like spirit would diffuse itself generally into the minds of the people of this country, but I despair of seeing it—some petitions were presented to the Assembly at its last Session, for the abolition of slavery, but they could scarcely obtain a reading. To set them afloat at once would, I really believe, be productive of much inconvenience & mischief; but by degrees it certainly might, & assuredly ought to be effected & that too by Legislative authority." Washington's letter seems to indicate that he felt gradual abolition would be the best way to end slavery in America. The letter also shows that it was clear to him that legislation to abolish slavery would not happen any time soon in Virginia.

~

Now that Washington no longer intended to sell the people he owned, he had to figure out how to balance his financial responsibilities.

His plantation needed to provide enough money to sustain his family's lifestyle. It also had to provide for the needs of hundreds of enslaved people. In good years, Washington's workforce produced what was needed for food and clothing, including fish, corn, textiles, and leather for shoes. In bad years, when the corn crop didn't produce enough, Washington had to purchase corn to keep everyone fed. As the years went by, problems like these made it more and more difficult for Washington to come out ahead financially.

Another drain on Washington's finances came from his mother, Mary Ball Washington. He supported his mother, yet she constantly asked him for money. In a letter to her on February 15, 1787, Washington bluntly explained the financial problems he faced, saying, "I have now demands upon me for more than 500£ three hundred and forty odd of which is due for the tax of 1786; and I know not where, or when I shall receive one shilling with which to pay it. In the last two years I made no Crops. In the first I was

George Washington created this map of his five farms: River Farm, Mansion House Farm, Union Farm, Dogue Run Farm, and Muddy Hole Farm. The area of the mansion is at the bottom near the middle.

obliged to buy Corn and this year have none to sell, and my wheat is so bad I cannot neither eat it myself nor sell it to others, and Tobaca I make none. Those who owe me money cannot or will not pay it."

When Washington was unanimously elected president in 1789, money was still an issue. Washington planned to take William Lee, Christopher Sheels, and others with him when he left for New York City, but he did not have enough money to pay for the trip. It was clear that he needed a loan in order to get to his own presidential inauguration.

On March 4, 1789, Washington wrote Richard Conway, a merchant and ship owner in Alexandria. He asked to borrow funds, explaining that his cash-flow problem stemmed from "Short Crops, & other causes not entirely within my Controul." Washington admitted that he had to do "what I never expected to be reduced to the necessity of doing—that is, to borrow money upon interest." On March 6, 1789, Washington borrowed £625 in Maryland currency at 6 percent interest. By the time Washington paid off his debt on December 15, 1790, with interest he paid more than £649.

~

During Washington's years as president, life for Peter Hardiman and Caroline went on as usual. Washington continued to rent Hardiman from Eleanor Custis Stuart for £12 a year. Hardiman, Caroline, and the other enslaved African Americans at Mount Vernon continued to have few choices in life. Another person owned them, their children, their parents, their siblings, and their friends. Someone else told them what to do, when to do it, and how to do it. Someone else selected and distributed the food they ate and the clothes that covered them. Someone else told them when to work and when to stop. They labored six days a week, year after year, for a lifetime.

Historians believe that through the years, some people who were enslaved used what is called "passive resistance," which is nonviolent opposition to those who had power over them. In order to have a small measure of control over their lives, some may have pretended to be ill, worked at an intentionally slow pace, stopped working when unsupervised, broken tools, misplaced tools, or left them out in the weather to be ruined. Since there is no documentation to prove passive resistance was occurring at Mount Vernon, no one will ever know for sure. But it seems Washington suspected this was happening.

From Philadelphia, Washington was keeping track of what was happening at Mount Vernon through his manager's weekly farm reports. The reports included a rundown of the work being done by Washington's enslaved people—including Peter Hardiman, who was expected to be useful in other ways when he wasn't busy with the care of horses and mules. When Washington didn't see Hardiman's work mentioned in the reports, he suspected idleness. He wrote his farm manager, Anthony Whitting, "If Peter does *any* work at all it is in the Gardening line . . . though I believe he will do nothing that he can avoid—of labour."

A few weeks later, on December 30, 1792, Washington wrote, "I have long suspected that Peter, under pretence of riding about the Plantations to look after the Mares, Mules, &ca is in pursuit of other objects; either of traffic or amusement, more advancive of his own pleasures than my benefit."

Washington also believed Caroline was not working hard enough. When she was not busy with her duties as a housemaid, Caroline also worked as a spinner, washer, knitter, and seamstress. Since Mount Vernon was as self-sufficient as possible, enslaved seamstresses made the clothes for every enslaved man, woman, and child on the plantation. It was slow work, done by hand. On December 23, 1792, Washington's letter to Whitting pointed out that the seamstresses produced "only Six shirts a week, and the last week Caroline (without being sick) made only five; Mrs Washington says their usual task was to make nine with Shoulder straps, & good sewing: tell them therefore from me, that what *has* been done, *shall* be done by fair or foul means; & they had better make choice of the first, for their own reputation, & for the sake of peace & quietness. otherwise they will be sent to the several Plantations, & be placed as common laborers under the Overseers thereat."

Was Caroline employing passive resistance? Or was something else going on? Was Caroline injured? Was she ill? Had she been up all night caring for a sick child? It is impossible to know. What we do know is that Washington was disappointed in her work. If she and the other seamstresses didn't produce the expected number of shirts per week, Washington threatened to send them to work in the fields.

These were not idle words. Slavery operated in large part on fear: the fear of physical punishment, fear of being sold away from your family, fear that your family would be sold away from you, and for the skilled workers like Caroline, fear of being sent to work in the fields at one of Washington's other farms. The enslaved community at Mount Vernon knew their master did not usually sell the people he owned, although he had on rare occasions in the past. They also knew he did not usually allow physical punishment. So at Mount Vernon, the most looming threat was being sent to the fields to work.

Most of the field workers were women, not men, who worked from daylight to dark. The majority were women because many of the enslaved men who lived near the mansion house were considered skilled labor—they were trained as carpenters, blacksmiths, coopers, cooks, valets, coach drivers, and more.

In the end, Caroline was not sent to work in the fields. But the threat would have always hung over her head.

~

Even as Washington was running the nation, he was troubled about more than idleness at his plantation. He could tell from Anthony Whitting's inventory reports that Mount Vernon's supply of hogs, wheat, nails, and tools was decreasing. After examining one report he realized that eight sheep were gone. Washington suspected his enslaved people were stealing them. On November 25, 1792, Washington wrote to Whitting that "half my Stock may be stolen, or eaten, before they are missed: whereas, a weekly, or even a more frequent Count of the Sheep, & inspection of the Hogs (articles most likely to be depredated upon) would prevent, or if not prevent, enable them to pursue while the scent was hot these atrocious villainies; and either bring them to light, or so alarm the perpetraters of them, as to make them less frequent. As the Overseers, I believe, conduct matters, a Sheep, or Hog or two, may, every week, be taken without suspicion of it for months. An enquiry then comes too late; and I shall have to submit to one robbery after another, until I shall have nothing left to be robbed of."

Washington was also concerned about safeguarding the linen that was used to make clothing for everyone on the plantation. On February 17, 1793, Washington cautioned his farm manager to beware of letting Caroline cut out the clothing pieces from the fabric. He suggested the hired gardener's wife should do it, because he felt that Caroline "was never celebrated for her honesty" and "would not be restrained by scruples of conscience, from taking a large toll [on the linen] if she thought it could be done with impunity."

In 1793, Caroline was given a new assignment on top of her usual duties. Anthony Whitting, the farm manager, fell seriously ill, and Caroline was ordered to take care of him. Just a few months before, Whitting had been the one to deliver the ultimatum to Caroline from the master: either produce the requisite number of shirts per week, or work in the fields. Whitting would have been the one to carry out the threat, if Washington had ordered it. For six days in March of 1793, Caroline tended to the man. She had no choice.

As Whitting's health deteriorated, goods continued to disappear from Mount Vernon. On May 19, 1793, Washington wrote Whitting that "it is indispensably necessary that a stop should be put to that Spirit of thieving & house breaking, which has got to such a height among my People, or their associates. As one step towards the accomplishment of which, I desire you will absolutely forbid the Slaves of others resorting to the Mansion house; Such only excepted as have wives or husbands there—or, such as you may particularly license from a knowledge of their being honest & well disposed—all others, after sufficient forewarning, punish whensoever you shall find them transgressing these orders." Whitting was not able to tend to these concerns, or to the overall management of Mount Vernon, much longer. Despite Caroline's efforts to aid him, he died on June 21, 1793.

Washington hired another farm manager, but the issue of missing goods continued, and as the years went by, the problem grew. Thieves broke into locked buildings like the smokehouse and corn loft. More and more supplies vanished, including alcohol, vegetables, meat, grain, milk, and butter. After a time, Washington suspected his enslaved people were not only stealing items from Mount Vernon, but selling them to others outside the plantation.

The problem of theft wasn't an issue unique to Mount Vernon. The same thing was happening on surrounding plantations. State laws were written to prevent stolen items from being sold. Any enslaved person who wished to sell their goods at the Sunday market in Alexandria now not only had to have a permit signed by their overseer that granted them permission to be there, they also had to have a signed certificate of approval stating that the goods being sold were not stolen property.

~

Throughout Washington's presidency, the family came home to Mount Vernon for periodic visits. Once the family arrived, even if their stay would only be for a few weeks, the house filled with guests. The extra mouths to feed were an advantage to Caroline in one way. On July 15, 1796, Caroline sold the Washingtons nineteen of the ducks she raised, all of which were no doubt destined for the dinner table.

The next day, July 16, one of the overnight guests was architect and artist Benjamin Henry Latrobe, who would later finish the U.S. Capitol building. In his journal, Latrobe detailed his stay at Mount Vernon. He also drew sketches of the house and grounds as he walked around the estate, as well as a profile of Washington.

At six o'clock that evening refreshments were served on the piazza. Latrobe drank coffee and visited with the Washingtons as the beautiful Potomac River rolled by in the distance. Latrobe preserved the moment in sketches.

Latrobe wrote about many things he

TOP: Benjamin Henry Latrobe visited Mount Vernon in 1796. He sketched scenes including this image of an enslaved person serving coffee on the piazza. Although no one will ever know for sure, it is possible the enslaved man pictured here is Frank Lee.

BOTTOM: This Benjamin Latrobe watercolor is based on the sketch he made during his visit to Mount Vernon. In this finished painting, Latrobe left out the enslaved man who was serving coffee to the Washington family.

Sketch of a groupe for a drawing of
see page 59.

encountered at Mount Vernon. He probably didn't see William Lee, who was busy making shoes, or Caroline slipping in and out cleaning rooms and emptying chamber pots, but he may well have observed Frank Lee, William Lee's brother, who worked in the house, or Christopher Sheels, dressed in livery and waiting for Washington's next order. But Benjamin Latrobe didn't mention in his account those he did see who silently worked in his midst. It was almost as though they were invisible.

~

When Washington's second term as president ended, the family returned to Mount Vernon. Although Caroline continued her work as a spinner and seamstress, her usual work in the mansion resumed too.

Many of the visitors who arrived were total strangers who wanted to see Washington, the most famous man in the world. Being at Washington's home was such an exciting experience that many guests wrote detailed accounts of their visits in letters and diaries.

One of the strangers who dropped by unannounced was Amariah Frost. Unlike Latrobe, who made no mention of the Washingtons' servants, Frost noted in his journal on June 26, 1797, "Our horses and the men who drove the carriage were taken suitable care of by his domesticks." It was Peter Hardiman who would have looked after Frost's horses. Frost was invited to stay for dinner that included roasted pig, leg of lamb, roasted fowl, peas, cucumbers, artichokes, pudding, and more.

So many visitors came to Mount Vernon that it was unusual for the family to dine alone. In a letter to Tobias Lear on July 31, 1797, Washington remarked on what would be a rare occasion, saying, "Unless some one pops in, unexpectedly, Mrs Washington and myself will do what I believe has not been [done] within the last twenty years by us, that is to set down to dinner by ourselves."

In 1798, there were 656 dinner guests at Mount Vernon and 677 overnight guests. In addition to the guests themselves, many arrived with their own servants. While the family must have grown tired of playing host to a constant crowd, and probably fretted over the cost, the Washingtons' enslaved people did the real work. For Caroline, visitors meant even more rooms to clean, more portable beds to prepare, more sheets to change, more clothes to launder, and more chamber pots to empty. The visitors never stopped, and neither did Caroline's labor.

One guest who arrived at Mount Vernon around this time was not expected by the Washingtons—or by Caroline. Seven-year-old Hannah Taylor and a friend were playing hide-and-seek in Alexandria when she hid in a coach that had been brought to the city for repairs. Waiting to be found, Hannah fell asleep. Meanwhile, the coachman took the coach back home—to Mount

These two bells mounted outside of Mount Vernon were part of a communication system. Some rooms inside the house had a wire that connected to a different bell—each having a different sound. The Washington family pulled a wire when they wanted to call one of their enslaved people. Caroline would always have been listening for a bell to summon her.

Vernon. Hannah woke up at Mount Vernon and screamed with fear. Washington sent a rider back to Alexandria to let her parents know she was safe and would be returned the next morning. After dinner that evening, it was Caroline whom Martha Washington called on to take the child upstairs and put her to bed. Caroline put embers from the fire into a warming pan and ran the pan up and down the sheets to heat them. She helped Hannah into one of Nelly Custis' nightgowns that had lace at the neck and sleeves. Then Caroline tucked Hannah into bed and left a candle burning until she drifted off to sleep. After breakfast the next morning, her mistress ordered Caroline to heat a brick for the coach to help keep the child warm on the trip home that snowy day.

~

Like his wife, Caroline, Peter Hardiman and the others who worked in the stable were kept extra busy with the arrival and departure of so many guests. They were tasked with the enormous responsibility of caring for and feeding the many horses that brought people to the Washingtons'—as well as caring for their equipment. When the guests departed, Hardiman would have saddled their horses or hitched them to a carriage, and prepared for whoever arrived next.

During the summer of 1798, a Polish writer named Julian Niemcewicz came to Mount Vernon and stayed twelve days. He noted details about Peter Hardiman and Washington's mule breeding operation. Niemcewicz wrote that the general kept up to fifty mules. He charged the public a $10 stud fee for his male donkeys Royal Gift or Knight of Malta to breed with their female horses. Niemcewicz wrote that in addition to the stud fee, each mare was charged for feed and "besides this a ½ doll. for the boy." The "boy" here was Peter Hardiman.

Julian Niemcewicz toured all over the Mount Vernon plantation during his stay. Unlike many others who chronicled their visits, Niemcewicz made mention of the enslaved people he saw there. Some of his accounts are rosy in their tone, such as his description of a group of people playing a game on their one day off. He wrote, "Either from habit, or from natural humor disposed to gaiety, I have never seen the Blacks sad. Last Sunday there were about thirty divided into two groups and playing at prisoner's base [a form of tag]. There were jumps and gambols [leaps] as if they had rested all week. I noticed that all spoke very good English."

Other observations were less upbeat, such as his description of the living quarters of one enslaved family: "We entered one of the huts of the Blacks, for one can not call them by the name of houses. They are more miserable than the most miserable of cottages of our peasants. The husband and wife sleep on a mean pallet, the children on the ground; a very bad fireplace, some utensils for cooking, but in the middle of this poverty some cups and a teapot." This description was likely of a hut on one of Washington's four outlying farms.

Despite any misgivings he may have had about the enslaved people's housing conditions at Mount Vernon, the Polish visitor enjoyed the Washingtons' Southern hospitality so much that he later reported feeling right at home on the plantation. He wrote, "I was not a stranger but a member of the family in this estimable house. They took care of me, of my linen, of my clothes, etc."

Though he didn't say so, it was enslaved people like Caroline and Peter Hardiman who actually took care of his necessities at Mount Vernon.

Chapter Four

Ona Maria Judge

Ona Maria (Oney) Judge was born in 1774, the same year George Washington took William Lee with him to the First Continental Congress in Philadelphia.

Her mother, Betty, had lived at Mount Vernon for fifteen years at the time of her daughter's birth. Betty and her son, Austin (Oney Judge's older half brother), were taken to the plantation when her mistress, Martha Custis, married George Washington in 1759.

Oney Judge's father was likely a white man named Andrew Judge. He was an indentured servant—someone who agreed to work for a period of time in exchange for ship's passage to America. Andrew Judge signed a four-year contract with Washington to work as a tailor. He arrived at Mount Vernon to begin his servitude in 1772.

Since Andrew Judge was a tailor and Betty a seamstress, they likely worked near each other. No records exist that tell us what sort of relationship Betty had with Andrew Judge. They may have loved each other. At a time when most enslaved people did not have a last name, it is significant that she named her daughter Oney Judge. In 1780, Betty had another daughter, named Philadelphia (Delphy) Judge. Andrew Judge stayed on to work at Mount Vernon for years after his indenture period was up. He left Mount Vernon around 1780. No records indicate that Andrew Judge stayed in contact with Betty or her daughters after that.

Since Betty was considered the property of Martha Washington's dower estate, each and every one of her children was too. Oney Judge was a freckle-faced ten-year-old

This Indenture Made the Eighth Day of July in the Year of our LORD GOD One Thouſand Seven Hundred & Seventy two BETWEEN Andrew Judge of the one Party, and Alex.r Colbelough Merch.t of the other Party, WITNESSETH, That the ſaid Andrew Judge doth hereby Covenant, Promiſe and Grant to and with the ſaid Alex.r Colbelough his Executors, Adminiſtrators and Aſſigns, from the Day of the Date hereof until the firſt and next Arrival at Baltimore or any port in America and after, for and during the Term of Four Years, to ſerve in ſuch Service and Employment as the ſaid Alex.r Colbelough or his Aſſigns ſhall there employ him according to the Cuſtom of that Country in the like Kind. IN CONSIDERATION whereof the ſaid Alex.r Colbelough doth hereby Covenant and Grant to and with the ſaid Andrew Judge to pay for his Paſſage, and to find and allow Meat, Drink, Apparel and Lodging, with other Neceſſaries during the ſaid Term. And at the End of the ſaid Term, to pay unto him the uſual Allowance according to the Cuſtom of the Country in the like Kind. IN WITNESS whereof the Parties abovementioned to theſe INDENTURES have interchangeably ſet their Hands and Seals, the Day and Year firſt above written.

Signed, Sealed and Delivered, in the Preſence of

Jno McDermott Lea
Mayor

Andrew his X mark Judge

1545

Oney Judge was probably the daughter of a white man named Andrew Judge. This is the indenture paper for Andrew Judge, where he agreed to work for four years in exchange for passage to America. When he arrived in America, George Washington bought his indenture, which contracted him to work for Washington for four years. Notice the signature at the bottom right: Andrew Judge signed his name with an X, which means he had not been taught to read or write. The person who filled out the document noted that the X was "his mark."

when she was sent to work inside the mansion house.

Even though Oney Judge was a child herself, she probably helped care for Martha Washington's two youngest grandchildren, who lived at Mount Vernon. She was about four years older than Nelly Custis and about six years older than G.W.P. Custis.

Judge's mother had taught her to be a highly skilled seamstress, and eventually she became Martha Washington's personal maid. As with the position of George Washington's valet, the demands on a lady's maid were constant. Judge got up before her mistress and worked long past the time she helped her get ready for bed.

As personal maid, one of her duties was helping dress and undress Martha Washington each day. There were many steps to the process. First she helped her mistress into a fresh white linen shift. Next she put stockings on her feet, smoothed them down, and tied them below the knee with garters to keep them up. Then she worked the whalebone corset over her mistress's head and pulled the strings to fit it nice and snug. She helped Martha Washington step into the petticoat that extended wide to each side, and tied it around her waist. After that she tied a pocket around her waist that could be accessed through a slit in her skirt. The skirt was next to go on, followed by the bodice of the dress, and then a triangular scarf was draped around the top of the dress to cover the low-cut bodice. Finally, Judge placed cloth shoes on her petite mistress's tiny feet, and buckled them.

At the end of the day, Oney Judge carefully reversed the process, piece by piece, before helping Martha Washington into her nightgown. Once she had her mistress settled for the night, Judge looked over each article of clothing carefully and wiped them with a dry cloth. If any of the expensive clothes were dirty or stained, she took them away for cleaning. She knew how to remove any sort of spot on the beautiful linen shifts, silk or muslin dresses, stockings, and shoes. If the gold and silver lace that decorated these clothes was dirty, Judge used talc and alcohol to rub them clean. She also saw to it that every article of clothing was neatly folded and ready for the next time they would be needed.

Martha Washington's role as mistress of the plantation was crucial. Although guests arrived to see her famous husband, it was Lady Washington who charmed them with her warmth, kindness, and friendly conversation. Judge stayed near during these visits—in the background but close enough to hear any order given by the woman who owned her.

The house was Martha Washington's domain and she supervised every detail. Although the lady of the house did not get up as early as her maid, she did rise each day before the sun. She oversaw breakfast preparations, and checked on those who were working at spinning and laundry and in the dairy. After breakfast she met with the cooks to choose the menu for dinner. In the late morning or early afternoon she gathered some young enslaved women to teach them how to sew and knit, and to create beautiful needlework and embroidery. She also oversaw the cutting of the fabric that would be made into clothing for the people at Mount Vernon. Since Judge had superb skills with a needle, she likely helped the younger girls as well.

Oney Judge was about fifteen years old when George Washington was elected president. She would continue as Martha Washington's personal maid in New York. But it would take some time for Washington to prepare her household for the move. The first lady, her grandchildren, and the enslaved people she planned to take with them would join the president after his inauguration.

When everything was finally packed and ready for the move in the spring of 1789, Oney Judge and the rest of Martha Washington's entourage left for New York. As the carriage pulled away from Mount Vernon,

Judge left most of her family behind—but she may have been comforted to know that her half brother, Austin, would be traveling north with her. Austin was at least seventeen years older than Judge.

May 27, 1789, was a special day. It was the day Lady Washington would join her husband, the very first president of the United States, in their official residence. That morning, Judge helped Martha Washington dress in a beautiful white gown and styled her hair.

Oney Judge was with her mistress when they arrived with great fanfare in Elizabethtown, New Jersey. President Washington and several other gentlemen met them there. The group then boarded the federal barge, and thirteen men rowed them toward Manhattan. When the barge passed the battery at the southern tip of the island, a salute was fired from a cannon to welcome Lady Washington to the capital city. Judge heard the boom of the cannon and felt the rumble. The barge turned up the East River and docked at Peck's Slip.

Oney Judge knew her master and mistress were important people. But on that day she also would have seen how dearly loved George and Martha Washington were. A huge crowd

This 1789 map (with inset) of the southern tip of what is now Manhattan shows the location of Peck's Slip, where Oney Judge and First Lady Martha Washington arrived to join President George Washington. To the right, just a couple of blocks away, is Cherry Street, the location of their first home in the city.

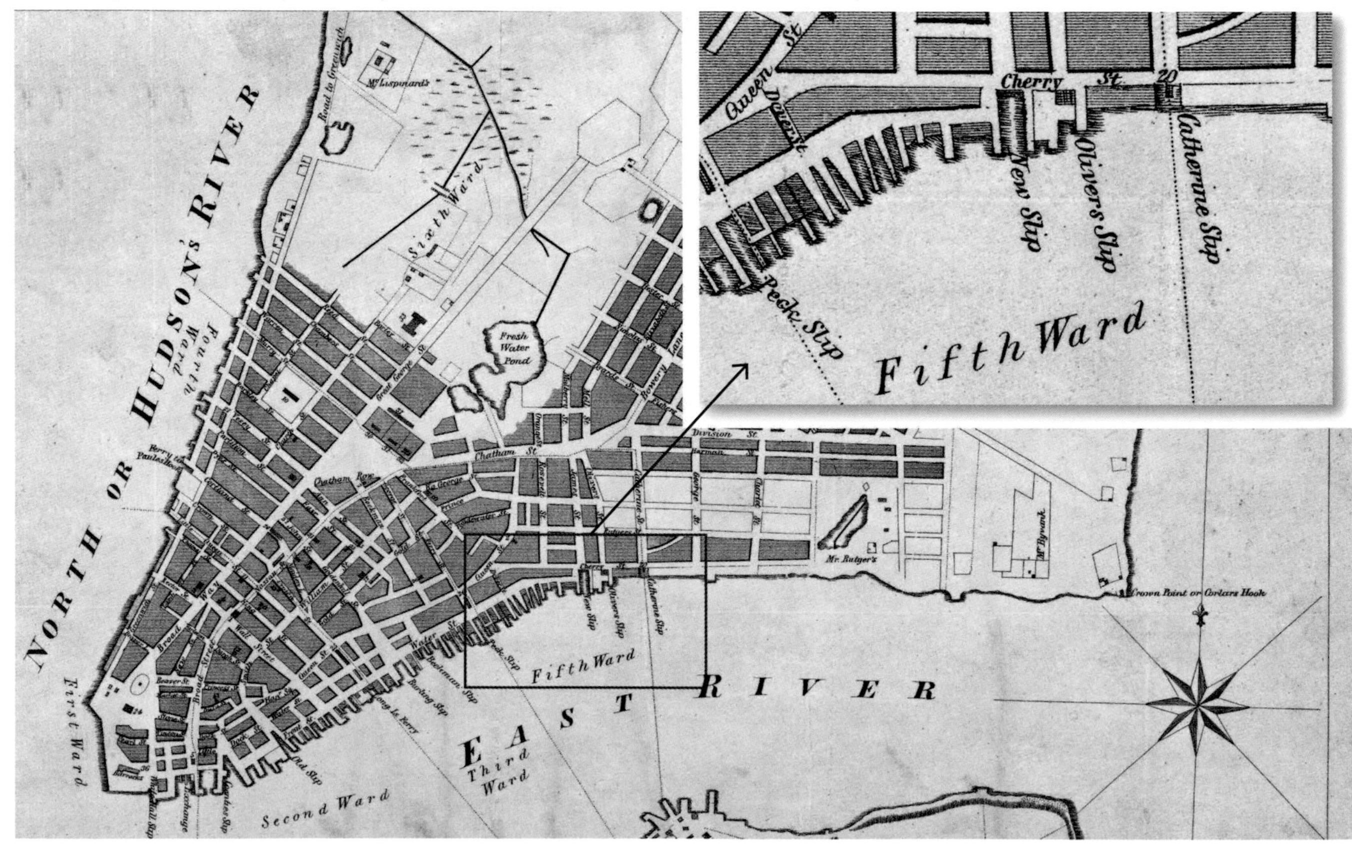

Oney Judge lived in the president's house at 3 Cherry Street in New York City. It was Washington's home and office for the first few months they were in the city. The house no longer exists; the spot where it stood is near the present-day footings of the Brooklyn Bridge.

of dignitaries had gathered to meet them. The most influential ladies in New York City welcomed the first lady of America. The governor of New York, George Clinton, led the way as the president, his wife, the grandchildren, and Oney Judge made the short walk to their new home at 3 Cherry Street.

Congress chose the residence on Cherry Street for the president's house and had it prepared for use as a home and for official functions. They expanded one of the drawing rooms to be used for entertaining, and appointed the house with beautiful mahogany furniture, Chinese porcelain, dishes, glassware, silver and silver-plated pieces, and luxurious window and bed hangings. When it was finished the house was elegant, but no more extravagant than the homes of wealthy people in New York.

Martha Washington's official duties as first lady began the evening after her arrival. Oney Judge helped her mistress dress for her first dinner, which was attended by foreign dignitaries from France and Spain, Vice President John Adams, the governor, and many other politicians. Every day after was a whirlwind of activities for Lady Washington—and for Judge. In addition to Washington's responsibilities as first lady, she was also busy getting her grandchildren settled into their new lives.

On June 8, 1789, Martha Washington wrote her niece Fanny Bassett Washington, "I have not had one half hour to myself since the day of my arrival." The same could likely be said of her maid, for when Martha was busy, Oney Judge was even busier.

Everything President Washington and Lady Washington did was noticed by the public. As the president's wife, Martha Washington had to dress in a way that befitted her station and her personality. While she was first lady, her clothes were simple in design, as they'd always been, but beautifully made from the very best materials. Since it was summer, Judge helped Martha Washington dress in cool white muslin gowns each day. Here at the president's house, just as at Mount Vernon, it fell to Judge to keep those clothes free of stains. She likely set her mistress's hair daily with a heated curling iron.

As Martha Washington's maid at Mount Vernon, Oney Judge herself had worn much nicer clothes than the rough ones issued once a year to most of the enslaved community. But now that national and international visitors would see her, she had to be dressed even better. Soon after they arrived in New York, her mistress ordered Judge several new gowns, stockings, and shoes. While her clothes were not made of silk like Martha Washington's, they were nevertheless beautiful dresses made from calico, linen, and soft lawn fabric.

The Washington family lived on Cherry Street for a few months, and then moved to a larger house on Broadway that better fit their needs. By the time Congress moved the capital of the United States to Philadelphia, the Washingtons and Oney Judge had lived in New York for about sixteen months.

This silk satin gown was worn by Martha Washington during the presidential years. It is the only one of Martha Washington's dresses to survive intact. Oney Judge would have dressed her mistress in this gown many times, and kept it clean. As was the fashion of the day, the low-cut bodice was filled in with a fichu (scarf).

Before relocating to Philadelphia, the Washingtons went home to Mount Vernon for a visit. When they set off for Pennsylvania, Oney Judge traveled with them. Senator Robert Morris, who signed both the Declaration of Independence and the Constitution, and who was considered the financial expert of the American Revolution, offered his home to be used as the president's house there. The large, four-story brick mansion was conveniently located at 190 Market Street (also called High Street), just one block from Congress Hall.

Oney Judge was not the only enslaved person from Mount Vernon to be taken to Philadelphia. Her older half brother, Austin, was there with her at the new presidential residence too, along with Christopher Sheels, Hercules, Richmond, Joe, Moll, Giles, and Paris. There were also many hired white workers on hand. Running the president's house took lots of people.

On February 22, 1791, George Washington's birthday, Martha Washington gave Oney, Austin, Moll, and Hercules one dollar each so they could buy gifts for their friends and family back at Mount Vernon. It would have been a unique experience for Oney to shop in the big city of Philadelphia for her mother and sister back home.

At the time, Philadelphia was the largest city in America. The population of the city itself was twenty-eight thousand people, but counting the suburbs there were about forty-two thousand in the area. Even after living in New York, Oney Judge may have been impressed by the harbor full of ships, tall buildings, huge churches, a library, the Pennsylvania State House, stores, theaters, and covered public markets.

As Judge accompanied the Washingtons around the bustling city or ran errands for them, she likely had more chances than ever before to make friends. Philadelphia was home to a great variety of people, including free blacks and abolitionists who supported the Gradual Abolition of Slavery Act and who worked to end slavery completely.

Oney Judge was one of the reasons why Attorney General Edmund Randolph came knocking at the front door of the president's house on Market Street on April 5, 1791. That was the day he paid his fateful visit to Lady Washington with a warning that some of the people he owned were claiming their freedom through the Gradual Abolition Act, and cautioned her that the enslaved men and women she and her husband had brought with them from Mount Vernon might do the same after living in Philadelphia for six months.

Soon after, Oney Judge was on her way to New Jersey with Christopher Sheels to serve Martha Washington while the first lady paid a social call. When they returned to Pennsylvania, the clock had been reset on the teenagers' six-month residency period in the state.

~

As the months passed in the president's house, Judge's wardrobe was continuously updated. Her mistress ordered chintz dresses, stockings, and cloth shoes for her maid. Judge wore these in the president's house when ladies visited, as well as when she accompanied Martha Washington on the first lady's social calls. She also accompanied Nelly Custis when she went visiting. One of Nelly Custis' dearest friends was Elizabeth Langdon, the daughter of John Langdon, a U.S. senator from New Hampshire. The two girls spent a lot of time together—so for Elizabeth Langdon, Oney Judge was a familiar face.

Although Judge was privy to the social interactions of both Martha Washington and Nelly Custis, as a lady's maid she was not there to socialize. Stylishly well-dressed Oney Judge likely sat quietly with her dark eyes and freckled face turned toward her needlework as she made delicate stitches. All the while, she would have been watching and waiting for her mistress's next order.

~

On June 5, 1792, the Washington family attended a performance in Philadelphia. Martha Washington enjoyed it so much that she gave Oney Judge, her half brother Austin, and Hercules money to see it too. The trio blended into the bustling crowd as they made their way down Market Street toward the Southwark Theater. They walked down the sidewalk while horse-drawn carriages clattered over the cobblestones. That night, a Frenchman named Alexander Placide delighted the crowd with a show that featured comedy, dancing, tightrope walkers, tumbling, and a balancing act.

The next year, the Washingtons enjoyed a new type of entertainment that was available for the first time in America: a circus. Again, they wanted Oney and some of their other enslaved people to experience it too. The show featured the amazing horsemanship skills and riding tricks of John Ricketts. He awed the audience as he rode his galloping horse on his knees and then jumped up over a ribbon twelve feet above the ground. He juggled four oranges while riding at full speed. Between his tricks came performances by a tightrope walker and funny clowns. For the grand finale, with his horse charging, Ricketts balanced with one foot on his saddle, while on his shoulder a boy stood on one foot.

These rare entertainment opportunities must have been temporary distractions for Judge. Yet life continued as it always had for her and the other enslaved staff at the president's house. For Washington's enslaved people, there was a glaring difference between them and the rest of the people who served there. Most of the individuals who worked at the president's house were paid white and free black workers from Philadelphia. Oney

Judge, Austin, and the others from Mount Vernon were not employees. The Washington family owned them.

Later in 1793, Washington was reelected and began his second term. The next year, just before Christmas, Austin was sent back to Mount Vernon for a brief trip. He traveled alone and stopped to spend the night at Harford, Maryland, at an inn owned by Mrs. Elizabeth Stiles. A hard rain pounded on the roof that night, and the downpour caused the water level in the nearby stream to rise to about three feet deep. Early the next morning, Austin saddled and mounted his horse to continue his journey. One of the enslaved boys from the inn waited near the stream just in case Austin's horse balked at going into the cold, moving water.

Austin urged his horse forward. In the middle of the stream Austin stopped so his mare could get a drink. Suddenly Austin dropped the reins, grabbed the horse's mane, and slumped over. The horse reacted by turning around. The movement threw Austin out of the saddle. He went underwater. The boy watching from the bank realized Austin's foot was caught in the stirrup, and he dashed through the water to help. Once he had pulled Austin's head above water, he screamed for assistance.

Help arrived and Austin was carried back to the inn. But he couldn't talk. Mrs. Stiles immediately called for the doctor, who believed Austin had suffered a stroke while on his horse. The doctor administered the only remedy he knew, which was to bleed Austin. But the treatment did not help.

Austin died at about one o'clock in the afternoon on December 20, 1794. He was in his late thirties or early forties. Mrs. Stiles arranged for a coffin to be built for him. After a funeral, Austin was buried in Harford.

Washington must have been known to hold Austin in high regard, since several different people wrote to tell the president exactly what happened. John Carlile, who had been a captain in the Continental Army during the Revolution, wrote that he believed the circumstances would be of interest to "an indulgent master."

Oney Judge was likely grief-stricken over Austin's death. Since her half brother was so much older than she, Austin may have been a father figure to her. She had no way to personally communicate with the rest of her family about Austin's death, since none of them had been taught to read or write. She could not have sent comforting words to her elderly mother, Betty, even if she had wanted to.

Despite her loss, Oney Judge carried on. More gowns, stockings, and shoes were ordered for her as the old ones grew worn. Every day she continued to help her mistress dress and undress, clean her mistress's clothes, set and dress her mistress's hair, place jewelry around her mistress's neck, serve her mistress tea, make social calls with her, run errands, and do needlework.

Judge wore beautiful clothes too, but none of them truly belonged to her. She lived in a luxurious house, but it wasn't her home. She walked down the street, but couldn't keep going and going if she wanted to. Martha Washington gave Judge many things, except the one thing she wanted: freedom.

In 1795, Oney Judge was twenty-one years old. She had worked as Martha Washington's personal maid for more than half her life. She knew her mistress well, as she did her mistress's grandchildren, Nelly and G.W.P. Custis, who lived with them. Judge also knew Martha Washington's two oldest granddaughters, Betsy and Patty Custis. These girls lived with their mother, Eleanor Custis Stuart, but spent a lot of time visiting Mount Vernon. When Betsy and Patty Custis were visiting Martha Washington, Judge probably served them just as she did their grandmother and their siblings.

Patty Custis married Thomas Peter early in 1795. A couple of months later, her sister Betsy Custis wrote her grandmother to ask if she could come to Philadelphia for a visit. With her younger sister married before her, Betsy Custis appears to have been depressed. On April 6, 1795, Martha Washington wrote to her niece Fanny Bassett Washington that Betsy Custis spent her time alone and took "no delight" in going out to visit people, attend functions, or go to church. She continued that her grandaughter "often complains of not being well—she took ill when she first came here—but is much better and looks better tho she does not like to be told so."

The next month, on May 12, 1795, Martha Washington wrote Fanny Bassett Washington, "Betsy you know is often complaining." Their grandmother mentioned that Betsy and Nelly Custis seemed to have no time to do their work, and that although they "stand at the window all day to look at what is doing in the street Betsy does not take much pleasure in going out to visit."

Later that year, the difficult Betsy Custis met Thomas Law. He was twice her age and had three sons. Early the next year George and Martha Washington were surprised to learn that Betsy Custis planned to marry Law. Before their marriage on March 21, 1796, the president wrote letters of congratulations and extended an invitation for the couple to visit them in Philadelphia.

It may have been during this honeymoon visit that Judge heard the horrible news: Martha Washington had decided that after her own death, Betsy Custis Law would inherit Judge.

Judge was two years older than Betsy Custis and had known her all her life. Judge knew the girl was sullen, lazy, and difficult. The thought of being owned by Betsy Custis Law was probably horrendous.

Oney Judge didn't want to be owned by anyone.

She wanted to be free.

Judge knew she had to escape.

But how?

~

As the summer of 1796 approached, the Washington family began planning their usual summer visit to Mount Vernon. It was Washington's final year as president, and this would be the last summer they would make a temporary visit to Mount Vernon. The next spring they would move back home permanently.

Oney Judge likely figured this was her best—and possibly only—chance to run. Having been in the president's house since the beginning, she knew what had happened to Christopher Sheels a few years before: the Washingtons had left Sheels at Mount Vernon after a trip home. Judge must have known that it was possible the Washingtons might leave her behind at Mount Vernon when they returned to Philadelphia for the last few months of Washington's presidency.

Escape from Mount Vernon in Virginia would be far more challenging than escaping from Pennsylvania. In Philadelphia, there were plenty of white abolitionists and free black friends to help her.

To succeed, Judge could not make the Washington family suspicious. She had to look as she always looked. She had to speak as she always spoke. She had to act as she always acted.

So, as usual, Oney Judge worked diligently to help prepare the Washington family for the trip back home. As usual, she packed her own belongings. Only this time, she had a different destination in mind for them. She made secret arrangements for her clothes to be taken to the home of a friend in Philadelphia. Their absence went unnoticed by anyone.

On May 21, 1796, as usual, the Washington family sat down for dinner at three o'clock. And that is when Oney Judge slipped out the door of the president's house. She blended into the Saturday afternoon crowd on Market Street and made her way toward the home of some free black friends in the city.

No one she passed on the street could have known what was going through Judge's mind. Was her heart pounding in her ears as each step took her farther and farther away? Did her pace quicken as she walked away from the main street? Was she tempted to glance back over her shoulder to see if she was followed? Did she cautiously look around the street to see who might recognize her? Did she have an alibi ready, an explanation for why she was out, if she was stopped? How long would it take before Martha Washington discovered she was gone?

Oney Judge reached her friends' house. At some point later that day, she made her way to the harbor. She headed for a single-masted sloop bound for Portsmouth, New Hampshire, named the *Nancy*, which was under the command of Captain John Bolles. When Judge boarded his ship, perhaps Captain Bolles knew exactly who his passenger was and why she was traveling alone. Perhaps he did not. Either way, he did not stop her.

Finally the ship set sail, leaving Philadelphia behind. When the *Nancy* reached the open sea the sail snapped as it caught the wind. Perhaps relief washed over Oney Judge in that moment. Perhaps the sun warmed her freckled face. Perhaps salty air whipped through her dark hair.

The trip from Philadelphia to Portsmouth took about five days. Oney Judge may have been filled with questions about her future. How could she support herself in New Hampshire? Would Washington search for her? What would happen if she was discovered?

In that moment, however, one thing was certain: she was free.

After Oney Judge disappeared, this runaway ad was published in the May 24, 1796, edition of the *Pennsylvania Gazette* in Philadelphia. Frederick Kitt was the steward, or manager, of Washington's presidential household.

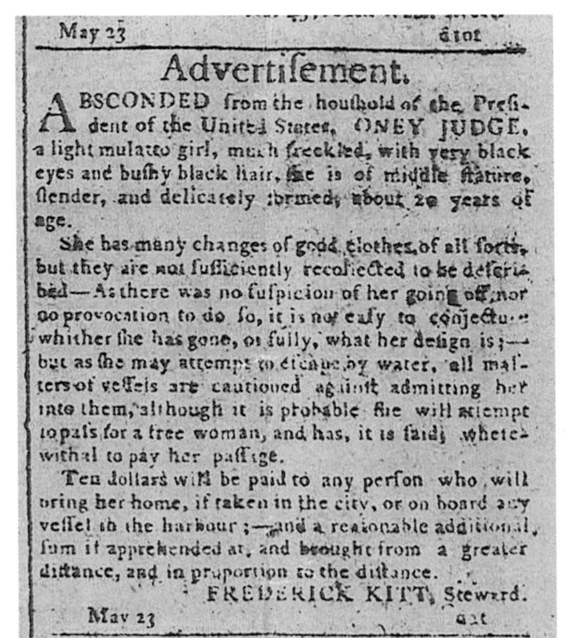

May 23 d10t

Advertiſement.

ABSCONDED from the houſhold of the Preſident of the United States, ONEY JUDGE, a light mulatto girl, much freckled, with very black eyes and buſhy black hair, ſhe is of middle ſtature, ſlender, and delicately formed, about 20 years of age.

She has many changes of good clothes, of all ſorts, but they are not ſufficiently recollected to be deſcribed—As there was no ſuſpicion of her going off, nor no provocation to do ſo, it is not eaſy to conjecture whither ſhe has gone, or fully, what her deſign is;—but as ſhe may attempt to eſcape by water, all maſters of veſſels are cautioned againſt admitting her into them, although it is probable ſhe will attempt to paſs for a free woman, and has, it is ſaid, wherewithal to pay her paſſage.

Ten dollars will be paid to any perſon who will bring her home, if taken in the city, or on board any veſſel in the harbour;—and a reaſonable additional ſum if apprehended at, and brought from a greater diſtance, and in proportion to the diſtance.

FREDERICK KITT, Steward.

May 23 d2t

~

Historical records show that Martha Washington was shocked and hurt when she discovered Oney Judge had run away. President Washington's surprise over her escape turned to determination to get his wife's property back. Shortly after her disappearance, Frederick Kitt, the steward of the president's house, placed a runaway-slave advertisement in the newspaper. It read:

"ABSCONDED from the household of the President of the United States, ONEY JUDGE, a light mulatto girl, much freckled, with very black eyes and bushy hair. She is of middle stature, slender, and delicately formed, about 20 years of age.

"She has many changes of good clothes, of all sorts, but they are not sufficiently recollected to be described—As there was no suspicion of her going off, nor no provocation to do so, it is not easy to conjecture whither she has gone, or fully, what her design is; but as she may attempt to escape by water, all masters of vessels are cautioned against admitting her into them, although it is probable she will attempt to pass for a free woman, and has, it is said, wherewithal to pay her passage.

"Ten dollars will be paid to any person who will bring her home, if taken in the city, or on board any vessel in the harbour;—and a reasonable additional sum if apprehended at, and brought from a greater distance, and in proportion to the distance.

"FREDERICK KITT, Steward.
May 23"

When word got out that Oney Judge had run away, reports of possible sightings were sent to the president. One said she had been seen in New York City. Another report claimed she was seen in Boston. Washington wasn't sure if any of the rumors were true. It seemed she had disappeared without a trace.

~

After Judge landed in Portsmouth, she lived there as a free woman and found work as a seamstress. But only a few months after she arrived, she was walking down the street when she spotted someone she knew—and who knew her. In fact, they knew each other well. It was Elizabeth Langdon, the dear friend of Nelly Custis, whose father was the senator and a friend of George Washington's.

Oney Judge saw Elizabeth Langdon. Elizabeth Langdon saw Oney Judge. Elizabeth stopped to talk—but Judge brushed past her and kept going. This was not a social call, as their previous encounters had been. Oney Judge was now a runaway and Elizabeth was a girl who could identify her.

Judge knew Elizabeth would tell her father. And soon, President Washington would know where she was.

Washington did indeed find out that Judge was in Portsmouth. On September 1, 1796, he wrote a letter to Oliver Wolcott Jr., his Secretary of the Treasury, explaining that Judge had "been the particular attendant on Mrs Washington since she was ten years old; and was handy & useful to her, being perfect Mistress of her needle." Washington asked Wolcott to ask the man who oversaw the port of Portsmouth to "recover and send her back."

President Washington considered Judge to be "simple and inoffensive" and unable to plan her own escape. He believed she was enticed away by a Frenchman. To Wolcott he explained, "It is certain the escape has been planned by some one who knew what he was about, & had the means to defray the expence of it & to entice her off." He ended his letter by saying, "I am sorry to give you, or any one else trouble on such a trifling occasion—but the ingratitude of the girl, who was brought up & treated more like a child than a servant (& Mrs Washington's desire to recover her) ought not to escape with impu[nity] if it can be avoided."

From Washington's perspective, he and his wife had treated Judge with care and kindness. To his mind, she had never been mistreated. She had never worked in the fields under the sweltering Virginia sun like most of the other enslaved women. She had been given nice gowns, bonnets, stockings, and cloth shoes to wear. She had lived in New York City and Philadelphia, where she attended various types of entertainment. George and Martha Washington couldn't imagine why she would want to run away.

Oney Judge's perspective was very different: Someone else owned her. She wanted to be free.

Wolcott did as the president asked and contacted the customs officer at Portsmouth, Joseph Whipple. On October 4, 1796, Whipple reported back to Wolcott on the situation. He'd found out that Judge was staying with friends, and booked passage for her on a sailing ship back to Philadelphia. Now he needed to speak with her.

Whipple approached Judge under the pretense of wanting to hire her to work in his home. But when he talked with her, Whipple dropped the charade and told her about Washington's letter and why he had come.

Judge told Whipple in no uncertain terms that she had not been enticed away by a French gentleman. Her only reason for escaping was "a thirst for compleat freedom."

Whipple wrote to Wolcott, saying that "she expressed great affection & Reverence for her Master & Mistress, and without hesitation declared her willingness to return & to serve with fidelity during the lives of the President & his Lady if she could be freed on their decease, should she outlive them, but that she should rather suffer death than return to Slavery & liable to be sold or given to any other person."

Judge's suggestion that she return to the Washingtons for the rest of their lives seemed reasonable to Whipple. He was sure the arrangement would be acceptable to the president. By the time Whipple left Judge that day, she'd agreed to return to Philadelphia aboard a ship that was leaving in a few hours, and assured Whipple that she would not tell her friends what she was planning to do.

But the weather turned bad that day and the ship was unable to sail. The next day, Judge's friends found out that she was planning to return to the Washingtons. There is no record of what her friends said to her that day. Perhaps they begged her not to go. Perhaps they questioned why she would want to return to slavery after escaping it. Perhaps they argued that Judge didn't know for sure that the Washingtons would free her after they died.

Whatever they said made a difference. Oney Judge did not board that ship.

Many runaways fled to New Hampshire. Whipple explained to Wolcott that the opinion of most in his state was "in favor of universal freedom." This meant it was difficult to send them back to their masters once they reached New Hampshire. Whipple had suggested that the president go through legal channels to "adopt such measures for returning her to her master as are authorized by the Constitution of the United States."

Oliver Wolcott shared Whipple's letter with George Washington. The president was not happy about it. In response to Whipple's suggestion that Judge be freed after their deaths, Washington wrote directly to Joseph Whipple, "To enter into such a compromise, as she has suggested to you, is totally inadmissible ... for however well disposed I might be to a gradual abolition, or even to an entire emancipation of that description of People (if the latter was itself practicable at this Moment) it would neither be politic or just, to reward unfaithfulness with a premature preference; and thereby discontent, beforehand, the minds of all her fellow Servants; who by their steady adherence, are far more deserving than herself, of favor."

Washington clarified that Judge's "conduct will be forgiven by her Mistress" if she returned with no expectation of being freed after their deaths. If Judge did not return, Washington wanted her to be "put on board a Vessel."

By this time, Washington had privately expressed his hope that legislation would one day abolish slavery, and he had decided not to buy or sell any more enslaved people. But his changing views on slavery did not influence how he felt about runaways—especially runaways from his own family. He was determined to hunt down any who dared escape. As long as slavery was legal, Washington would control his property and the property of his wife as he saw fit. He absolutely would not make a deal with Oney Judge, no matter how much his wife wanted her back. To his way of thinking, to make an agreement with Judge would be rewarding a runaway. And that could cause unrest in the whole of his enslaved community.

Another factor, of course, that Washington had to consider was the fact that since Judge was one of the people who was owned by his wife's dower estate, even Martha Washington could not free her. She had to remain in the Custis family after Martha Washington's death, whether she was inherited by Betsy Custis or someone else.

Judge's escape put Washington in a difficult position. When she disappeared, Washington reacted as a slave owner and posted a runaway ad in the newspaper. But he was no ordinary citizen; he was the president of the United States. Washington had political enemies who would use any sort of scandal against him. While he wanted to get Judge back, the president didn't want to create a scene.

Washington wanted Judge to be put on a ship, but he explained to Whipple that he did not "mean however, by this request, that such violent measures should be used as would excite a mob or riot, which might be the case if she has adherents, or even uneasy sensations in the minds of well disposed Citizens."

Washington would rather let Judge go than make a deal with her, or cause a public scandal.

When Whipple answered President Washington on December 22, 1796, he explained that no ships were ready to depart for either Alexandria or Philadelphia. Whipple also wrote that Judge had applied for a license to marry a free biracial man.

In early January 1797, Samuel Haven performed the wedding of Oney Judge and John (Jack) Staines, who was a sailor. Their marriage was recorded by the town clerk in Greenland, New Hampshire, and announced in the January 14 edition of the *New Hampshire Gazette*.

Oney Judge Staines lived like an emancipated woman. But deep down, she knew she wasn't completely free. Even though she'd successfully escaped from her mistress, even though she was married to a free man, legally she belonged to Martha Washington's dower estate.

As months turned to years Martha Washington still missed Oney Judge and wanted her back. Two years after she escaped—and probably at his wife's insistence—Washington attempted once more to get her back. On August 11, 1799, Washington wrote his nephew Burwell Bassett Jr. that if he could recover the runaway it would "be a pleasing circumstance to your Aunt." He cautioned Bassett not to do anything that would be "unpleasant, or troublesome" in his efforts to retrieve her. Washington clarified again that if she returned, Judge would not be punished for running away. But she would not be freed.

When Bassett found Oney Judge Staines, her husband was away at sea. By this time she had a child, a daughter named Eliza. If Bassett couldn't get Oney Judge Staines to go voluntarily, he planned to take her and her child by force. He was staying as a guest in the home of John Langdon and his daughter Elizabeth, the young woman who had recognized Oney Judge on the street in Portsmouth. But when Bassett told Senator Langdon his plans, Langdon sent a secret messenger to Oney Judge Staines. He warned her to leave the city by midnight, or she would be taken back to Mount Vernon.

Terror must have gripped her when she heard this message. She had to get away, and she had to hide her daughter, who legally belonged to Martha Washington's estate. It didn't matter that Oney Judge Staines had been living for three years as a free woman five hundred miles from Mount Vernon. Bassett could come for her and her child at any moment.

With no time to lose, Oney Judge Staines took Eliza and ran to a stable to hire a boy with a horse and carriage. With her husband away, she left for the home of her free black friends, Phyllis and John Jack. The Jack family lived eight miles away in Greenland, New Hampshire.

Bassett didn't know where she had gone.

Once again, Oney Judge Staines disappeared without a trace.

CHAPTER FIVE

Hercules

When Hercules was a boy he was assigned to work the ferry. He rowed people back and forth across the Potomac River for John Posey, his master. Posey owned a plantation named Rover's Delight that bordered Mount Vernon. As Hercules rowed the ferry across the river day after day, he couldn't have known that his owner had money problems—or that very soon those problems would directly affect him.

John Posey had borrowed a lot of money from his neighbor George Washington, and didn't have the money to repay him. In an effort to settle a small part of what he owned Washington, Posey offered to sell him twenty-six African Americans for the deeply discounted price of £70.

On October 22, 1765, long before Washington's views on slavery began to shift, he bought eleven-year-old Hercules and twenty-five other human beings.

Four years after Hercules was purchased by Washington, Posey still owed Washington some money. In order to raise enough to pay his debt, Posey sold all of his possessions,

Hercules was first owned by John Posey, whose name is on this remnant of a wine bottle found in the trash pit at Mount Vernon during an archaeological dig. Gentlemen would sometimes order bottles of wine with their names on them. In the eighteenth century, the letter "s" was sometimes written or printed in a way that looks like an "f" without the crossbar.

including the ferry, his two-hundred-acre farm, and "twenty-five choice SLAVES, consisting of men, women, and children. Also sundry horses, cattle, sheep, and hogs." To settle his accounts, all the money John Posey got from selling his "chattel"—the personal property he owned—went to George Washington.

Once the ferry across the Potomac River belonged to George Washington, he sent Hercules to work on it again. In 1770 Hercules showed up for the first time on Washington's taxable list as one of the "Ferry men." Slave owners did not pay taxes on enslaved children until they turned sixteen. Once they reached sixteen their owners included them on a "list of tithables" and paid tax on them.

By the next year seventeen-year-old Hercules was working as a house servant in the Mount Vernon mansion alongside Doll, William Lee, Frank Lee, Giles, and others. Since Hercules would be seen every day by the Washington family and their guests, he wore a coat, waistcoat, and breeches.

While still in his teens, Hercules married an enslaved girl who worked as a housemaid and seamstress. She was listed in Mount Vernon's property records as "Lame Alice." Alice was a popular name for women at Mount Vernon, and it was not uncommon for people with the same name to be differentiated by their physical characteristics, often in terms that are now outdated. Alice was owned by Martha Washington's dower estate. Hercules belonged to George Washington. Hercules and Alice had their first child in February of 1771. It is likely the child did not survive, since there is no record of the baby being named.

At the end of November 1777, Hercules and Alice brought into the world a son whom they named Richmond. At the time of Richmond's birth, the master of Mount Vernon was facing major problems. General Washington had been away fighting the Revolutionary War for about two years. The Continental Army under his command was on the brink of total collapse. The British army occupied the capital city of Philadelphia. General Washington was about to lead his men to winter quarters at Valley Forge, Pennsylvania. Many of his men marched through the snow in bare feet, and didn't have enough clothes to keep them warm or food to keep them fed.

But General Washington managed to keep his army together through Valley Forge and eventually the rest of the war. Finally in 1783 the war officially ended and Washington returned home with William Lee. That same year, Hercules and Alice welcomed into their family a daughter, Eve, who would later be listed as a "dwarf." Two years later another daughter was born, whom they named Delia.

Alice died in September 1787, and may have been buried in the slave cemetery near the mansion. She left behind Hercules and their three children. Richmond was ten years old, Eve was four, and Delia was two.

The year before his wife's death, Hercules went to work in the kitchen, helping the aging cook, Old Doll. Another man, named Nathan, joined Hercules in the kitchen. The two young men learned much from Christopher Sheels' grandmother as they assisted her. It took great skill to keep the oak or hickory fire burning in the massive kitchen fireplace. She taught them how to roast meat using the rotating spit over the fire's embers, and how to prepare fish the way Washington liked it. Old Doll taught them how to control the heat in the brick oven to cook bread, cakes, and cookies. Hercules learned, and his skills as a chef grew and grew.

~

G.W.P. and Nelly Custis knew Hercules well and called him "Uncle Harkless." G.W.P. Custis later described Hercules as "a dark-brown man, little, if any, above the usual size, yet possessed of such great muscular power as to entitle him to be compared with his namesake of fabulous history."

Hercules had been working as a cook for about four years when President Washington and his family prepared to move to

Hercules learned to cook in this kitchen at Mount Vernon. It took great skill to control the heat from a wood fire in order to cook a wide variety of dishes.

Cooks at Mount Vernon used this wooden bowl. You can still see the cut marks made while preparing food for the Washington family.

Philadelphia. Washington planned to hire a cook for the massive responsibility of working in the busy kitchen of the president of the United States. The salary would be $12 per month. Other perks of the position included food and a place to live.

Tobias Lear asked friends in Philadelphia for recommendations for a cook to hire. He also ran newspaper ads that said, "No one need apply who is not perfect in the business, and can bring indubitable testimonials of sobriety, honesty, and attention to the duties of the station." Not one cook was found who could meet the requirements.

By September of 1790, Washington was considering either Hercules or Nathan for the position. In November he decided to take Hercules with him to the capital city to work as cook. Hercules had no choice in the matter, and since he was Washington's property, he would not be paid $12 per month.

With his wife deceased, Hercules was the only parent left for his three children. His daughters were now seven and five years old. While he was gone, others within the Mount Vernon enslaved community would care for them. But Richmond was thirteen, the age when children went to work. Hercules asked Washington for permission to take Richmond with him to work in the kitchen.

Washington allowed it, but with reluctance. On November 22, 1790, Washington wrote Tobias Lear that he permitted Richmond to go "not from his appearance or merits I fear, but because he was the Son of Herculas & his desire to have him as an assistant, comes as a Scullion for the Kitchen."

Hercules arrived in Philadelphia along with others, including Christopher Sheels, Oney Judge, Austin, Moll, and Giles. New shirts, breeches, and a hat were ordered for Hercules now that he worked in the president's house.

On the days Hercules left the residence, the sights he took in weren't like anything he would have seen at Mount Vernon. In Philadelphia there were all kinds of entertainment, public buildings, taverns, inns, and stores filled with all manner of goods. The city streets were full of people, including foreign dignitaries, wealthy aristocrats, poor people, white abolitionists, and free black people.

In the president's house, where Washington's enslaved people worked alongside paid white servants, Sam Fraunces was the steward and manager of the kitchen. Hercules was the chief cook. According to G.W.P. Custis, Hercules was "as highly accomplished a proficient in the culinary art as could be found in the United States."

Philadelphia was the new capital city of the United States, but it was also the culinary capital of America. Cooks from Europe arrived, bringing with them their own distinct talents. The smell of cinnamon was in the air as German bakers turned out sticky buns. Chefs from France who had fled the French Revolution offered sweet pastries and ice cream. Poor black street vendors from the Caribbean cooked and sold ladles full of pepper pot soup, a hot and spicy dish with the flavors of the islands.

The harbor bustled with ships arriving with their cargo of foods like limes, coconuts, bananas, plantains, guavas, and pineapples. Spices from the West Indies, raisins from the Canary Islands, and olives and Gruyère cheese from France were unloaded in Philadelphia. Some ships sold massive green turtles—some as large as seventy pounds—which were used to make a local favorite, turtle soup. Locally grown and imported foods were for sale at the High Street Market, an impressive covered market less than two blocks from the president's house.

~

As chief cook in the kitchen of the president of the United States, thirty-six-year-old Hercules had the great responsibility of supervising workers to make sure every cooking utensil was shined and every table was spotless. The entire presidential household, black and white, free and enslaved, held Hercules in high esteem. G.W.P. Custis wrote that "the whole household, treated the chief cook with much respect, as well for his valuable services as for his general good character and pleasing manners."

Hercules settled into a routine as he worked as the chief cook in the kitchen of the president's house. He was an excellent chef and hard worker, and Washington knew it. When the steward, Sam Fraunces, suggested Washington rehire a white woman named Mrs. Read, Washington would not hear of it. She had been an unsatisfactory employee when they lived in New York City. He wrote Lear that "Herculas can answer every purpose that Mrs Read would do, and others which she will not."

Hercules' duties as chief cook came with a huge advantage: it gave him the privilege of selling the "slops" from the kitchen. This included anything that would not be consumed in the president's house, such as used tea leaves (used once and dried out), animal skin, feathers, and fat. Hercules made between one hundred and two hundred dollars a year from selling kitchen slops.

As they did for all the others at the president's house, the Washingtons supplied Hercules with new clothes when needed. But when Hercules had his own money to spend,

Hercules would have shopped at the High Street Market for food to put on the president's dinner table. This is one of the three covered markets, each a block long, that on market days would be filled with vendors selling all sorts of products.

he bought even finer clothes for himself. He purchased a black silk jacket, waistcoat, and breeches. His white shirts were made from the highest-quality linen. He bought silk stockings, and his shoes were polished to a shine and fastened with large buckles. In his memoir, G.W.P. Custis recalled Hercules' attire as a "blue cloth coat with velvet collar and bright metal buttons, a long watch-chain dangling from his fob, a cocked-hat, and a gold-headed cane completed the grand costume of the celebrated dandy."

Every Thursday night, members of Congress came to dinner at the president's house. The amount of food Hercules and the kitchen staff cooked was enormous. One week they prepared and served 293 pounds of beef, 111 pounds of veal, 54 pounds of mutton, 129 pounds of lamb, 16 pounds of pork, 44 chickens, 22 pigeons, 4 ducks, 10 lobsters, 98 pounds of butter, and 32 dozen eggs—plus lots of vegetables, fruits, cheeses, drinks, and desserts.

Hercules was at the very top of his game as he prepared the weekly state dinner. He barked orders to his staff that were immediately obeyed. G. W. P. Custis wrote that it was while preparing these dinners that Hercules "shone in all his splendor. . . . It was surprising the order and discipline that was observed in so bustling a scene. His underlings flew in all directions to execute his orders, while he. . . seemed to be everywhere at the same moment." Under Hercules' watchful eye, meats turned on the spit and various dishes bubbled in cast-iron pots hanging on hooks over glowing embers. Dutch ovens with coals heaped on the lids cooked others. Cooking began long before dawn, and it took all day to prepare the two dozen or so dishes of soup, meat, poultry, fish, vegetables, jellies, cakes, puddings, and more.

When the Washingtons' dinner guests arrived, they sat down in walnut chairs with crimson-upholstered seats. White dishes trimmed in gold gleamed in the candlelight at each place setting. Down the center of the table ran a long mirror tray that held delicate white porcelain figures made in France. Four or five servants dressed in livery stood waiting to serve the impressive dinner Hercules had worked on all day. The steward, Sam Fraunces, oversaw every detail of the formal dinner in the State Dining Room. He dressed in silk and wore a fresh white apron, and his hair was powdered. Dinner began precisely at 4:00 p.m.

On the nights of the weekly state dinners, Hercules' work was over as soon as the meal

Hercules was the chief cook in the president's house at 190 High Street (now Market Street) in Philadelphia. This house had served as headquarters for the British commander, Sir William Howe, while the enemy occupied Philadelphia, and later as Benedict Arnold's headquarters before he turned traitor. The house no longer exists. Today the Liberty Bell stands just a few steps from the location of the slave quarters where Hercules lived.

began. Once Fraunces took over the dinner service, Hercules went to the slave quarters and changed into his fine clothes. Immaculately dressed for the evening, Hercules made his way to the front door of the president's house. The doorman opened the door and bowed low to Hercules. He returned the bow to the doorman. Hercules strolled down Market Street, where people of every class congregated to visit. G.W.P. Custis later wrote about those who met Hercules while on his walks, and observed, "Many were not a little surprised on beholding so extraordinary a personage, while others who knew him would make a formal and respectful bow, that they might receive in return the salute of one of the most polished gentlemen."

~

Hercules worked hard. Some felt that his son, Richmond, did not. When Washington was away on his tour of the Southern states, Tobias Lear wrote him on April 1, 1791, that "nothing can be expected from Richmond—he is an idle ignorant boy, and they tell me (I believe with truth) that he is of no manner of service there."

Martha Washington was the mistress of the Washington family home regardless of whether they were in Virginia or Pennsylvania, and like her husband, she expected everyone to work hard no matter whether they were black or white, free or enslaved. She determined that Richmond should be sent back to Mount Vernon permanently. The first lady may have discussed her decision with Hercules, because in a letter to Washington, Lear wrote that Mrs. Washington "intended to send Richmond home by the first opportunity which will be about next Wednesday. Hercules is perfectly willing that he should go."

The decision to send Richmond home came around the same time that Edmund Randolph visited Martha Washington to discuss the fact that his enslaved people were claiming their freedom. Although most of the Washingtons' enslaved people who went with them to Philadelphia were owned by Martha Washington's dower estate, George Washington owned Hercules. To prevent Hercules from claiming his freedom through the Gradual Abolition of Slavery Act, he would have to be taken out of Pennsylvania for at least one day.

Martha Washington was planning to return to Mount Vernon the following month, but it would be after the six-month residency period had passed. It was at that point that Washington suggested to Lear that Hercules could be sent home by stage—before his wife left.

On April 24, 1791, Lear wrote Washington that "Richmond goes in a Vessel that sails tomorrow for Alexandria—and I shall propose to Hercules, as he will be wanted at home in June when you return there, to take an early opportunity of going thither, as his services here can now be very well dispenced with, and by being at home before your arrival he will have it in his power to see his friends—make every necessary preparation in his Kitchen & as he must return when you do to this place. . . . If Hercules should decline the offer which will be made him of going home, it will be a pretty strong proof of his intention to take the advantage of the law at the expiration of six months. As Mrs Washington does not incline to go to Virginia until you return to this place, the foregoing arrangement is the best I can think of to accomplish this business."

Neither Martha Washington nor Tobias Lear ordered Hercules to go, although they could have. Hercules probably understood the situation. Perhaps he was not fooled by the deceptive tactics of the Washingtons such as the trip to New Jersey that took Oney Judge and Christopher Sheels out of the state.

By May 22, 1791, Hercules was the only one of the enslaved people who worked for Washington in Philadelphia who had been there constantly for nearly six months. Lear wrote Washington that he recommended to Hercules that he "go home this week in the Stage, as there is no vessel now up, which he has promised to do, and I shall accordingly make arrangements for his departure."

But Hercules did not leave on the stagecoach.

On June 5, 1791, Lear wrote Washington and explained that when Hercules "was about to go, somebody, I presume, insinuated to him that the motive for sending him home so long before you was expected there, was to prevent his taking the advantage of a six months residence in this place. When he was possessed of this idea he appeared to be extremely unhappy—and altho' he made not the least objection to going; yet, he said he was mortified to the last degree to think that a suspicion could be entertained of his fidelity or attachment to you. and so much did the poor fellow's feelings appear to be touched that it left no doubt of his sincerity—and to shew him that there were no apprehensions of that kind entertained of him, Mrs Washington told him he should not go at that time; but might remain 'till the expiration of six months and then go home—to prepare for your arrival there. He has accordingly continued here 'till this time, and tomorrow takes his departure for Virginia."

Hercules missed his chance to legally claim his freedom. He stayed in Philadelphia until Martha Washington went home to Mount Vernon in the fall of 1791.

~

As Washington's first term as president neared an end, he looked forward to going home. He had no plans to try to stay in office. But many believed that if Washington left the presidency, bitter political parties would tear the country apart. Reluctantly, Washington agreed to run for a second term as president. In late 1792, Washington was unanimously reelected by the Electoral College—and

Hercules learned to cook in Mount Vernon's kitchen, the building at the top right. He and other enslaved men pounded sandstone to make the sand that was used to rusticate the main house, the kitchen, and the servant's hall—the building seen in the foreground. In the winter of 1797, Hercules cut blocks of ice from the frozen Potomac River (behind the mansion) and stored them in the icehouse. Ice kept like this lasted into the summer and allowed the Washington family the luxury of ice cream and cool drinks on hot days.

Hercules continued his hectic schedule. It was physically grueling work, and house records show that Hercules required liniment and medicine in January and February 1795.

Eventually Hercules was taken back to Mount Vernon, but it is unknown exactly when. Historical records show that in February of 1795 Hercules was in Philadelphia—but by November 1796 he was back at the plantation, and no longer working as a cook. While Hercules had been in Philadelphia, others cooked at Mount Vernon.

One event that occurred between those dates may have been a factor in the decision for Hercules to return to Virginia: Oney Judge ran away on May 21, 1796. Perhaps Washington decided to take Hercules back to Mount Vernon to prevent him from doing the same thing—but no one will ever know for sure.

From Philadelphia in the fall of 1796, Washington began assessing what needed to be done to his plantation in preparation for his return after his second presidential term was complete. One priority was to repaint the mansion. The outside of the house was covered with rusticated wood. To achieve the look, workers painted the wood and then threw sand on the wet paint to give it the appearance of stone.

When the house was rusticated years before, Washington used sand from the Chesapeake Bay. This time he wanted to experiment to see if the natural sandstone found on his own property would work just as well. To test it meant sandstone rocks had to be pounded into sand. It would be a lot of work to crush enough sandstone to use on the house, but Washington owned many people. On November 5, 1796, Washington wrote his farm manager, James Anderson: "If it shall be found, on experiment, that the pounded Stone answers as well, as sand for coating the houses, Frank, Herculas [Hercules] and Cyrus may get a good deal of it pounded. They may get up a large quantity of gravel at the place I shewed you."

When the Washingtons were at Mount Vernon, Hercules and Frank Lee's duties were in the kitchen and mansion. Cyrus worked both in the house and in the stable. But Washington had no need for them to work in those places when the family was not at home. That fall, after the three men had finished with the stone, Washington ordered them to dig enough clay out of the ground to make one hundred thousand bricks. They were also to assist the gardener with the hedges surrounding the house, and spread dung in the garden for fertilizer. Washington wrote, "In short let them be employed in any manner at, or near the M. House that will Keep them out of idleness & mischief."

Hercules' life back at Mount Vernon could not have been more different than it had been in Philadelphia. For six years he had been the chef who cooked world-class state dinners for the president of the United States. He had bought and worn fine clothes. He had strolled down the streets of Philadelphia and exchanged bows of respect and courtesy with those he met.

But now, all he'd experienced in Philadelphia was gone. Back at Mount Vernon, Hercules was pounding sandstone, digging clay, and spreading manure.

~

Hercules was reunited with his children when he returned to Mount Vernon. It had been five years since his son Richmond had been sent home from Philadelphia. In that time, Richmond had gone from working with his father in the kitchen to working on an outlying farm.

Hercules was back at Mount Vernon when nineteen-year-old Richmond got into serious trouble. Richmond stole money out of a saddlebag that belonged to a man named James Wilkes, a hired white servant who had worked in the presidential mansion. When Washington found out about the theft, he sent a letter to his farm manager, William Pearce, on November 14, 1796, writing, "I hope Richmond was made an example of, for the Robbery he committed on Wilkes Saddle bags." It is likely that "made an example of" meant that Richmond was whipped as punishment for his crime. Washington did not routinely permit the use of physical punishment, but he did allow it when he felt it was necessary. On November 15, 1796, the farm manager noted in the household account book that the "ten dollars & a Quarter that had been stolen by Richmon from James Wlks" was repaid.

In his letter of the 14th, Washington expressed his concern that Richmond's thievery might have been connected to the recent return of Hercules. He wrote, "I wish he may not have been put upon it by his father (although I never had any suspicion of the honesty of the latter) for the purpose perhaps of a journey together." It is unclear exactly when and why Washington began to suspect Hercules might try to escape and take Richmond with him. Washington told his farm manager not to mention his suspicions to anyone. But he cautioned Pearce to closely watch Richmond and Hercules.

On December 18, 1796, Washington's letter to his farm manager included his frustration that the gardener was not accomplishing the tasks asked of him. At the end of the letter he wrote, "P.S. What has Frank Herculas & Cyrus been employed in. No mention is made of any work performed by them in the gardeners or other Reports."

When the manager answered Washington he told his boss exactly what work Hercules accomplished during the week of January 1–7, 1797. That week Hercules cut roof shingles out of timber, and filled the icehouse with huge blocks of ice cut from the frozen Potomac River. It was a bitterly cold week, when the temperature rose above freezing only twice. On the two warmest days the temperature was 36 degrees and 38 degrees.

During the next two weeks, Hercules uprooted unwanted plants from the garden and planted others. In the last week of January, Hercules worked three days digging gravel. In early February, Hercules spent twelve days digging clay out of the ground to be used for making bricks.

And then, on February 22, 1797, Hercules was gone.

He ran away from Mount Vernon without a trace—on George Washington's birthday. He left everyone behind, including his three children, Richmond, Eve, and Delia.

No one knows how Hercules got away or where he went.

He just vanished. Hercules was free.

In the farm report dated February 25, 1797, the farm manager listed what the enslaved people at Mount Vernon accomplished during their six-day workweek. Two days that week Hercules was listed as digging clay. For the other four days, the manager wrote: "Herculees absconded."

Hercules may have intentionally chosen to leave on the day when the nation celebrated his master's birth. He picked a good time to run away, because the Washington family was in transition. Washington's two terms as president were over, and John Adams had been elected as the next president. The family was still in Philadelphia but was packing to move back home to Mount Vernon.

Washington had heard that Hercules was gone by the time the family left Philadelphia on March 9, 1797. The next day Washington wrote Tobias Lear a letter full of details about a new carpet for the parlor. Then he added one line about his runaway cook. He suspected Hercules would go to Philadelphia, so Washington wanted his house steward, Frederick Kitt, "to make all the enquiry he can after Hercules, and send him round in the Vessel if he can be discovered & apprehended."

The Washingtons returned home on March 15, and the visitors started coming. Some of the first were Louis Philippe (who became the king of France in 1830) and his two brothers. They arrived at Mount Vernon on April 5, 1797, for a four-day stay. The French noblemen were aware of the fact that Hercules had run away. In his journal Louis Philippe wrote that when his servant spoke to the daughter of Hercules, probably Eve, and "said to this little girl that she must be very sad not to see her father any more, she replied, 'Oh! sir, I am very glad, because he is free now.'"

George and Martha Washington missed Hercules' culinary skills. His years as the chief cook in Philadelphia had taught him how to prepare superb meals for large groups of people. But Hercules had run away, and none of the other cooks at Mount Vernon were up to the task.

More than ten years earlier, on September 9, 1786, Washington wrote John Mercer that he did not intend to purchase another person "unless some particular circumstances should compel me to it." It seems the disappearance of Hercules was one of those circumstances, as Washington was willing to buy another enslaved person if necessary in order to find a good cook who could handle the work at Mount Vernon. His nephew Bushrod Washington wrote Washington that there was a man known to be an excellent cook who was about to be sold in Fredericksburg. But the man had a "fondness for liquor."

On November 13, 1797, Washington wrote his nephew George Lewis that "the running off of my Cook, has been a most inconvenient thing to this family; and what renders it more disagreeable, is, that I had resolved never to become the master of another Slave by purchase; but this resolution I fear I must break."

In the end, Washington did not purchase another enslaved individual. He hired a white Englishwoman named Eleanor Forbes to oversee the house and kitchen staff. After Old Doll was too feeble to work, Lucy, the wife of Frank Lee (and William Lee's sister-in-law), had taken over the cooking at Mount Vernon.

Even though Washington had a cook, he still wanted to recover Hercules. On January 10, 1798, nearly a year after Hercules disappeared, Washington wrote Frederick Kitt in Philadelphia:

"We have never heard of Herculas our Cook since he left this; but little doubt remains in my mind of his having gone to Philadelphia, and may yet be found there, if proper measures were employed to discover (unsuspectedly, so as not to alarm him) where his haunts are.

"If you could accomplish this for me, it would render me an acceptable service as I neither have, nor can get a good Cook to hire, and am disinclined to hold another slave by purchase.

"If by indirect enquiries of those who know Herculas, you should learn that he is in the City, inform Colo. Clemt Biddle thereof, and he will, I hope, take proper measures to have him apprehended at the moment one of the Packets for Alexandria is about to Sale, and put him therein, to be conveyed hither; and will pay any expence which may be incurred in the execution of this business; which must be managed with address to give it a chance of Success—for if Herculas was to get the least hint of the design he would elude all your vigilance."

Kitt wrote back on January 15, 1798, "Since your departure I have been making distant enquiries about Herculas but did not till about four weeks ago hear anything of him and that was only that [he] was in town neither do I yet know where he is, and that will be very difficult to find out in the secret manner necessary to be observed on the occasion. I shall however use the utmost exertions in my power, and hereafter inform you of my success."

Hercules was never found.

CHAPTER SIX

The End of an Era

George Washington continued having money problems even after two terms as president. It was getting more and more difficult for Mount Vernon to sustain itself. From Washington's view, the numbers weren't good. By 1799, there were 317 enslaved people living at Mount Vernon. Washington provided food, clothes, and medical care to all of them. Of the 317, 132 were either too old or too young to work. This meant that only 58 percent of them were contributing to the plantation's production.

But in fact, the enslaved people who were able to work were too numerous. Washington didn't need that many laborers to keep Mount Vernon running, but their population grew as more and more babies were born.

Most plantation owners who owned more people than they needed or could afford opted to sell some of them—even if that meant separating husbands, wives, and children. But Washington would not do that, so his financial challenges grew along with the enslaved community.

Washington wrote to his nephew Robert Lewis about his situation on August 17, 1799:

"It is demonstratively clear, that on this Estate (Mount Vernon) I have more working Negros by a full moiety [half], than can be employed to any advantage in the farming System; and I shall never turn Planter thereon.

"To sell the overplus I cannot, because I am principled against this kind of traffic in the human species. To hire them out, is almost as bad, because they could not be disposed of in families to any advantage, and to disperse the families I have an aversion. What then is to be done? Something must, or I shall be ruined; for all the money (in addition to what I raise by Crops, and rents) that have been *received* for Lands, sold within the last four years, to the amount of Fifty thousand dollars, has scarcely been able to keep me a float."

~

Money problems were not the only issues George Washington wrestled with during the summer of 1799. Another struggle revolved around one question: What would happen to the enslaved people at Mount Vernon after he and his wife died? The time had come to make some decisions.

George Washington was the master of all 317 enslaved African Americans who served his family at Mount Vernon, but he didn't own all of them. He owned 123 people. He rented 41 people who were owned by others, including Peter Hardiman. And 153 people were owned by Martha Washington's dower estate.

For forty years, the entire population at Mount Vernon had lived together as one community. Couples fell in love and married regardless of whether they were owned by Washington, were rented from someone else, or were "dower slaves." While each person knew who owned them, it hadn't seemed to matter.

By 1799, it *did* matter to whom everyone belonged.

A heartbreaking division was coming to the enslaved community of Mount Vernon, and neither of the Washingtons had the power to stop it. This division would separate people who belonged to Martha Custis Washington's dower estate from those who belonged to George Washington. The great division was inevitable because of the inheritance laws of Virginia that did not permit Martha Washington to free the enslaved people who were part of her third of her late husband's estate.

Instead, since Martha Washington had four living grandchildren, the enslaved men, women, and children who were part of her dower's share of the estate would be divided among the four of them at her death. Once each of Martha Washington's grandchildren

Around June of 1799 Washington compiled a list of enslaved people at Mount Vernon that he titled "Negros Belonging to George Washington in his own right and by marriage." At the end of the "GW" column on the left is William Lee: "Will . . . Shoem [shoemaker], lame, no wife."

In the "Dower" column on the right, the fourth name is Wilson, son of Caroline and Peter Hardiman: "Wilson, ditto, 15, no wife." ("Ditto" here means Wilson had the same duty as Cyrus, whose name appears above his.) Farther down the list are the names of Caroline and Delphy (sister of Oney Judge).

On the right side at the bottom, above the "Children" heading, are the names of Hercules' two daughters, "Eve 17 ditto—a dwarf" and "Delia 14 ditto her sister." (Here the "ditto" for both Eve and Delia means neither had a husband.)

List
Negros
Belonging to George Washington in his own right and by Marriage

G.W

Names.	ages	Remarks
Tradesmen &c.		
Nat . . Smith		His wife . Lucy . D.R. . do.
George . . Do.		Ditto . . Lydia R.T. Do.
Isaac . Carpr.		. . . . . . Kitty Dairy Do.
James . . Do. .	40	. . . . Darcus M.H. C.W
Sambo . Do.		. . . . agnes. R.T. do.
Davy . Do.		. . . . Edy . U.T. C.W
Joe . . . Do.		. . . . Dolshy Spinr. do.
Tom . Coopr.		. . . . Nanny M.Ho. C.W
Moses . Do.	. .	No Wife
Jacob . . . Do.		. Ditto
George . Gardr.		His wife Sall . D.R. . do.
Harry . Do.		No wife
Boatswain Ditto		His wife Myrtilla Spinr. C.W
Dundee . Do.		His wife at Mr. Lears
Charles . Do.		Ditto . . Fanny U.F. do.
Ben . . Do.		Ditto . . Penny R.T. C.W
Ben . . Miller		Ditto . . Sinah . Mn. H. do.
Forester Do.		No Wife . .
Nathan . Cook	31.	Wife . . Peg . M.Ho. C.W
Wm. Muclus B.layr.		Do. . . Capt. Marshalls
Juba . Carter		No wife.
Matilda Spinner		Boson . Ditcher
Frank . Ho. Servt.		Wife . Lucy . Cook
Will . . . Shoem.		Lame . no wife
amount	24	

Names	ages	Remarks
Mansion House		
Payed Labour		
Frank . . .	80	No Wife
Gunner . . .	90	Wife . Judy . R.T. C.W
Sam . Cook	40	Ditto . Alce . M.H. Do.
amount . .	3	

Dower

Names.	ages	Remarks
Tradesmen &c.		
Tom Davis B.layr.		wife at Mr. Lears
Simms . . . Carp.		Do. Daphne . French's
Cyrus . . . Postn.		Do. Lucy . R.T. . . C.W
Wilson . Ditto	15	no wife
Godfrey . Cartr.		Wife . . Mima . Mn. Ho. do.
James . . Do.		Do. . . Alla . Do. . Do.
Hanson . . Distr.		No wife . . .
Peter . . . Do.		Ditto
Nat . . . Do.		Ditto
Daniel . Do.		Ditto
Timothy . Do.		
Ha: Joe . Ditchr.		Wife Sylla D.R . C.W
Christ . . . Ho. Ser.		Do. . Majr. Wests
Marcus . . Do.		No Wife
Lucy . . Cook		Husbd. Ho. Frank . . C.W
Charlotte . Sempst. (Patty written above Charlotte)		No Husband (written above No husband)
		No husband
Sall . . . Ho. Md.		Do.
Caroline . Do.		Husbd. Peter Hardman
Kitty . . . Milk Md.		Do. . Isaac Carpr. C.W
Alce . . Spinr.		Charles . Freeman
Betty Davis . Do.		Mrs. Washington's . Dick
Dolshy		Husbd. Joe . Carpr. C.W
Anna		Do. lives at George Town
Judy	21	No Husband
Delphy		Ditto . Do.
Peter . Lame Knittr.		No wife
Alla . . . Do.		Husbd. James Cartr. do.
amount	28.	

Names	ages	Remarks
Mansion House		
Will		Wife aggy D.R. C.W
Joe . Postilr.		Do. Sall . R.T. Do.
Mike		No wife . son to Lucy
Sinah		Husbd. Miller Ben . C.W
Mima		Do. Godfrey Wag. do.
Lucy		No Husband.
Grace		Husbd. Mr. Lear's . Jul.
Letty		No . husband
Nancy		Ditto . Do.
Viner		Ditto . Do.
Eve	17	Ditto . a dwarf
Delia	12	Ditto . her sister
Children		
Phil		son to Lucy
Patty		daughter to Do.

took ownership of their one-fourth shares of the men, women, and children, they would move them to their own homes—away from Mount Vernon.

~

About five years earlier it seems Washington may have considered how to avoid this great division. Instead of inheriting the people, perhaps the Custis heirs would accept their value in cash. What if Washington could buy them from his wife's grandchildren? The monetary value of every individual enslaved person depended on his or her gender, age, and skills. Mary V. Thompson, a research historian at Mount Vernon, has estimated that in 1799 the value of the 153 people owned by Martha Washington's estate was around £6,055, which at the time equaled $25,007.15 (approximately $647,000 today).

There was one familiar problem: Washington didn't have enough money. He owned tens of thousands of acres of land, but he didn't have cash. Washington tried to sell about thirty-three thousand acres of land west of Virginia. He wrote a letter to Tobias Lear on May 6, 1794, explaining that he wanted to turn his land into cash in part because he wanted the rest of his life to "be more tranquil & freer from cares." Along with this letter Washington wrote a separate note which he marked "Private" where he added another reason he wanted to raise some money: "I have another motive which makes me earnestly wish for the accomplishment of these things—it is indeed more powerful than all the rest—namely to liberate a certain species of property which I possess, very repugnantly to my own feelings; but which imperious necessity compels; & until I can substitute some other expedient, by which expences not in my power to avoid (however well disposed I may be to do it) can be defrayed."

Washington could not find a buyer for his land. Without cash he could not compensate his wife's grandchildren for the value of the enslaved people they were to inherit. By the summer of 1799, there was nothing he could do to stop the people belonging to Martha Washington's dower estate from being divided after her death.

~

At this point Washington planned to leave most of his own estate, including Mount Vernon, to his nephew Bushrod Washington, a Supreme Court justice. The law gave Washington the power to bequeath his property to Bushrod or to anyone else he wanted. If he gave the 123 enslaved people he owned to his nephew, it would guarantee their continued enslavement and the enslavement of their descendants for generations to come.

But Washington had another option. He could manumit (free) the people he owned. That would guarantee their liberty, as well as the liberty of their children and their children's children. Thompson estimated that in

1799 the value of the 123 enslaved people owned by George Washington was around £4,640, which at the time equaled $19,163.20 (approximately $495,000 today).

George Washington knew what he had to do.

On July 9, 1799, the sixty-seven-year-old former president sat down at the desk in his office. He had made his decisions. It was time to record them in a legally binding will that would replace his previous one. Washington picked up his quill, dipped it into the inkwell, and began to write.

"Upon the decease of my wife, it is my Will & desire that all the Slaves which I hold in my *own right*, shall receive their freedom. To emancipate them during her life, would, tho' earnestly wished by me, be attended with such insuperable difficulties on account of their intermixture by Marriages with the Dower Negroes, as to excite the most painful sensations, if not disagreeable consequences from the latter . . . it not being in my power, under the tenure by which the Dower Negroes are held, to manumit them."

Washington was planning ahead for two separate events: one was his own death, and the other was the death of his wife. Each of their deaths would bring major changes to the enslaved community at Mount Vernon, but in different ways. When Martha Washington died, those owned by her dower estate would be divided among her heirs. But according to Washington's new will, the 123 people he owned were to be freed—after his wife died.

By delaying manumission until after her death, Washington was putting his concerns for his wife's peace of mind before the liberty of the people he owned. He hoped to protect his wife from having to deal with the separation of men and women at Mount Vernon, which was sure to bring heartache to the married couples that were owned by different people. If Washington owned a wife and her children, they would be freed; but if the husband were owned by Martha Washington's dower estate, he would remain enslaved. And the opposite was also true. If Washington owned a man who was a husband and father, the man would be freed; but if the man's wife and children were owned by his wife's dower estate, they would remain in slavery. The situation raised many questions. Would the children of these families get to see both parents? Where would the freed people live? What sort of paying jobs could they get?

Washington anticipated the challenges that would face some of the people once they were free. He planned to provide help for those who would need it most. The people he owned who were elderly or had physical problems would be clothed and fed by his heirs during their lifetimes. He ordered a fund to be created to support them as long as any required it. Children who did not have parents, or had parents who were unable or unwilling to care for them, would be watched over by the court. The children were free, but as they grew up they would be bound to a master and mistress who had to teach them to read and train them for an occupation. At the age of twenty-five the children would be released and would have the life skills needed to provide for themselves.

Washington wrote, "I do herby expressly forbid the Sale" of any of his freed population. He prohibited any of them from being transported out of Virginia "under any pretence whatsoever." Washington made it clear that he intended those he had owned to be completely free. Perhaps he wanted to insure that no one would try to keep them bound in slavery by finding a loophole in the law—as he and his wife had done in Philadelphia.

Surrounded by the books in his office, Washington continued writing his instructions. The next ones involved William Lee:

"And to my Mulatto man William (calling himself William Lee) I give immediate freedom; or if he should prefer it (on account of the accidents which have befallen him, and which have rendered him incapable of walking or of any active employment) to remain in the situation he now is, it shall be optional in him to do so: In either case however, I allow him an annuity of thirty dollars during his natural life, which shall be independent of the victuals and cloaths he has been accustomed to receive, if he chuses the last alternative; but in full, with his freedom, if he prefers the first; & this I give him as a testimony of my sense of his attachment to me, and for his faithful services during the Revolutionary War."

Washington never forgot Lee's constant loyalty to him throughout eight years of war. Lee was the only one of Washington's enslaved people who was to be freed immediately upon Washington's passing, without waiting for Martha Washington's death. Washington wished to provide him with $30 a year for the rest of his life, and the freedom to either leave Mount Vernon or continue to live there. If he stayed, he would continue to be supplied with food and clothes.

Once Washington finished writing his will, he put it in his desk alongside his earlier will, and closed the drawer.

~

On December 12, 1799, just over five months after he wrote his updated will, Washington rode out to oversee his farms as usual. The weather turned nasty during his five-hour ride. A cold wind whipped around, bringing

Beginning on line six, George Washington's handwritten will says, "And to my Mulatto man William (calling himself William Lee) I give immediate freedom." Lee was the only one of Washington's enslaved people who was to receive his freedom upon Washington's death.

the aged and infirm;—seeing that a regular and permanent fund be establish
ed for their support so long as there are
subjects requiring it;—not trusting to
the uncertain provision to be made by
individuals.—And to my Mulatto
man William (calling himself William
Lee) I give immediate freedom; or if
he should prefer it (on account of the
accidents which have befallen him, and
which have rendered him incapable of
walking or of any active employment)
to remain in the situation he now is,
it shall be optional in him to do so: In
either case however, I allow him an
annuity of thirty dollars during his
natural life, which shall be indepen
dent of the victuals & cloaths he has
been accustomed to receive, if he chuses
the last alternative; but in full, with
his freedom, if he prefers the first;—& this
I give him as a testimony of my sense
of his attachment to me, and for his
faithful services during the Revoluti
onary War.—

Item To the Trustees (Governors, or by what
soever other name they may be designated)
of the Academy in the Town of Alexan
dria, I give and bequeath, in Trust,
four thousand dollars, or in other
words twenty of the shares which I

G° W[illegible]

with it rain, hail, and snow. He was late getting back for dinner at three o'clock. He went straight to the dining room to eat without changing clothes. The next day he had a cold and sore throat. During the middle of the night, Washington felt worse.

At daybreak on December 14, 1799, Caroline went into the Washingtons' bedroom to light a fire. Martha Washington told Caroline to go get Tobias Lear. By the time Lear arrived, Washington was having trouble breathing and could barely speak. Lear immediately sent for Dr. Craik. Washington communicated to Lear to send for Mr. Rawlins, one of the overseers, to bleed him before the doctor arrived. When Dr. Craik arrived he began administering the known medical treatments of the day including breathing in steam, a throat gargle, and bleeding him again. They sent for two more doctors.

Christopher Sheels stayed beside Washington. At eight o'clock that morning Washington wanted to sit up for a couple of hours. Sheels likely helped him dress and sit in a chair by the fire in his bedroom. About two hours later, Sheels helped him back to bed.

Sheels stood by the bed as the doctors bled Washington several times. He stood by the bed as the doctors gave his master medicines they hoped would help.

Hours dragged by. It became more difficult for Washington to speak. That afternoon, Washington realized his valet had been standing by his bedside for a long time and motioned for Sheels to sit in a nearby chair. Christopher Sheels sat down to rest.

Later that afternoon, Sheels helped Washington sit in a chair again. After about a half hour, Washington wanted to go back to his four-poster bed. Sheels likely helped him out of his clothes and back into his bedclothes.

As the afternoon dragged on, it was clear that Washington's condition was critical. About four thirty that afternoon he beckoned to his wife. He told her to go to his study and look in the drawer where he kept his two wills.

Martha Washington went down the stairs outside their bedroom and into her husband's study. In a drawer she found the two legal documents her husband had written himself. She climbed the stairs again, carrying both sets of papers. She entered the bedroom she had shared with her husband for forty years, and handed him the documents.

George Washington knew he was dying. He now had to make sure one of the two wills was destroyed so there would be no question about what he wanted to happen to his possessions.

The will he'd prepared years before may have left his property—including the people he owned—to his nephew.

The other will, the one he'd prepared just

months before, left clear instructions that after the death of his wife all of the people he owned were to be freed.

Freedom or slavery. Washington held in his hands the fate of 123 people and the generations that would follow them.

Washington considered each document. Then he handed one to his wife, and told her to burn it.

Martha Washington walked to the fireplace on the far side of the bedroom and placed the papers in the flames. The words on them curled and turned to ash.

Sometime after ten o'clock that night, George Washington died. Martha Washington sat at the foot of the bed. Dr. Craik and Tobias Lear were at his side. Christopher Sheels was standing by his master's bedside when George Washington took his last breath. Caroline and the other housemaids, Molly and Charlotte, stood in the room near the door.

Martha Washington told Sheels to give the contents of her husband's pockets to Tobias Lear. Sheels handed Lear Washington's keys and handkerchief. About midnight, Christopher Sheels probably helped the other men carry George Washington's body down the stairs of his beloved Mount Vernon for the last time.

Martha Washington took the will her husband chose to preserve and put it in her closet for safekeeping.

It was the document he wrote that summer. Upon her death, the men, women, and children he had enslaved would be free.

~

On December 18, 1799, a crowd of people gathered for George Washington's funeral. Pallbearers carried the coffin. The two grooms, Cyrus and Wilson (the son of Caroline and Peter Hardiman), led Washington's riderless horse, outfitted with his saddle, holsters, and pistols.

After the service, refreshments were served to the guests. According to Tobias Lear, after the guests had eaten their fill "the remains of the provisions were distributed among the blacks."

The words and feelings of family, friends, and the nation regarding Washington's death are well documented. The words and feelings of Mount Vernon's enslaved community regarding Washington's death are unknown.

One thing was certain, however. Nothing at Mount Vernon would ever be the same.

~

Martha Washington, devastated by her husband's death, moved out of the bedroom they had shared for forty years and into a small room on the third floor. One of Washington's nephews, Judge Bushrod Washington, who would inherit Mount Vernon after Martha Washington's death, was one of the executors of his uncle's will. Bushrod advised his aunt to get "clear of her negroes & of plantation cares & troubles."

In a room at the top of the mansion, the mistress of Mount Vernon mourned her husband and the life she had known.

In the slave quarters, some may have rejoiced and planned for a life they had never known—and something they could only have dreamed of.

Freedom.

∾

The people who had been owned by George Washington would be emancipated—just as soon as Martha Washington died.

George Washington had hoped to spare his wife from witnessing the separation of families by postponing their liberation until her death. But he did not anticipate the difficult position his decision would put her in. Very soon, Martha Washington understood that many people were anxiously awaiting her passing, and she feared some might want to speed it up. Rumors of poison and a possible house fire circulated.

It did not take long for Martha Washington to decide to free the African American people who had been owned by her husband.

George Washington had been gone for

MARCUS,

One of the House Servants at Mount Vernon,

ABSCONDED on the ſecond inſtant, and ſince has not been heard of. He is a young lad, about 16 years of age, a bright mulatto, dark blue eyes, long back hair, about 5 feet 4 or 5 inches high, and of a ſlender make. He had on when he left this place a coat and jacket of dark mixture, black and white, and black breeches—but having various ſuits, one of black, and another of very light drab, it is uncertain which of theſe he now wears. Originally his name was Billy, and poſſibly he may reſume the ſame. It is very probable he may attempt to paſs for one of thoſe negroes that did belong to the late Gen. Waſhington, and whom Mrs. Waſhington intends in the fall of this year to liberate—the public are therefore warned againſt any ſuch impoſition, as he is one of thoſe negroes which belong to the eſtate of Waſhington P. Cuſtis, Eſq. and held by right of dower by Mrs. Waſhington during her life.

I will give Ten Dollars Reward to any perſon who ſhall apprehend the ſaid negro and lodge him in ſome ſafe gaol, upon producing me a certificate to that effect; and will alſo pay all reaſonable charges over and above this reward, for the delivery of him to me at this place.

Ship Maſters are hereby forewarned not to take on board Marcus; and thoſe who are found to ſecret or harbour him, will be puniſhed as the law directs.

JAMES ANDERSON.

Mount Vernon, April 11——2t

Marcus, who belonged to Martha Washington's dower estate, understood that Washington's will did not free him. This runaway ad for Marcus suggests he planned to pass himself off as one of the people Washington freed. Marcus never retuned to Mount Vernon.

less than two months when the *Spectator*, a newspaper in New York, reported on February 1, 1800, that "Mrs. Washington has announced, that after this year all the negroes are to be emancipated. According to the General's wishes."

About a year after Washington's death, in December 1800, Martha Washington signed the manumission papers that freed his enslaved people. G.W.P. Custis later wrote, "The slaves were left to be emancipated at the death of Mrs. Washington; but it was found necessary (for *prudential* reasons) to give them their freedom in one year after the general's decease."

Martha Washington worried about what would happen to the people she had emancipated. About that time, Abigail Adams, wife of President John Adams, visited her old friend Martha Washington. Abigail Adams wrote a letter to her sister describing the situation at Mount Vernon:

"Mrs. Washington with all her fortune finds it difficult to support her family, which consists of three hundred slaves—one hundred and fifty of them are now to be liberated. Men with wives & young children who have never seen an acre beyond the farm are now about to quit it, and go adrift into the world without horse Home or Friend. Mrs. Washington is distrest for them. At her own expence she has cloathd them all, and very many of them are already miserable at the thought of their Lot. The aged she retains at their request; but she is distrest for the fate of the others. She feels as parent or wife. Many of those who are liberated have married with what are called the dower Negroes, so that they quit all their connections, yet what could she do. In the state in which they were left by the General, to be free at her death, she did not feel as tho her Life was safe in their Hands, many of whom would be told that it was [in] there interest to get rid of her—She therefore was advised to set them all free at the close of the year."

William Lee was free immediately when Washington died. The remaining 122 people owned by Washington were freed on January 1, 1801.

On May 22, 1802, Martha Washington died. Most of the people in her dower estate had lived at Mount Vernon all their lives. As the law dictated, everything she had inherited from her first husband, Daniel Parke Custis, passed to her four grandchildren. Her property included personal items, furniture, land, and 153 human beings.

The inevitable moment of the division had come. Four lists were made, one for each of the four Custis heirs. On each page were the names of the enslaved people they would inherit. The monetary value of each human being was listed beside their name. Christopher Sheels, who was a skilled, strong young man, was listed at £120. Doll (probably

Sheels' grandmother, Old Doll), who was too old to work, was listed at £5.

The people who had lived together as a community were separated. Those who would remain enslaved were moved to other plantations to begin serving new owners.

Upon Martha Washington's death, the enslaved men, women, and children who were part of her dower estate were divided up among her four grandchildren. This is a list of the enslaved people who were inherited by George Washington Parke (G.W.P.) Custis, and their monetary value. Caroline is No. 1 on the list. The eight names numbered 2 through 9 are the children of Caroline and Peter Hardiman. No. 15 is Christopher (Sheels). No. 18 is Doll (Old Doll).

Mr G. W. P. Custis's List of Slaves

No.	Name	Value
1	Caroline	£70
2	Wilson	£80
3	Rachael	£50
4	Jemima	£40
5	Leanthe	£35
6	Polly	£30
7	Brandum	£35
8	Austin	£25
9	Daniel	£20
10	Charlotte	£60
11	Elve	£60
12	Eliza	£25
13	Tim	£70
14	Phill	9?
15	Christopher	£120
16	Judy	£70
17	Louisa	£15
18	Doll	5
19	Sall (old)	15
20	Billy	£25
21	Cirus	£100
~~22~~	~~Hetty~~	~~20~~
22	Sam	5
23	Peter	5
24	Betty Davis	£60
25	Nancy	£50
26	Anna	£35
27	Lucinda	£20
28	Molly	£40
29	Grace	£60
30	Roger	£60
31	Peg	£50
32	Billy	£50
33	Peggy	£15
34	Daniel	£100
35	David	50
36	Will (old)	
708	66	

CHAPTER SEVEN

And Then What Happened?

WILLIAM LEE

With his newfound freedom following the death of George Washington, William Lee could have walked away from Mount Vernon and lived as a free man somewhere else. But he chose to stay at the plantation. Just as Washington had instructed, Lee received money from his master's estate for the rest of his life.

Lee was there when Martha Washington freed the remaining 122 people who had belonged to her husband, rather than wait until after her own death. He was there to see most of them drift away from Mount Vernon to begin new lives as free men, women, and children. Just as Washington had instructed, his elderly enslaved people were given a pension to support them for the rest of their lives. By the time the last one died, in the 1830s, Washington's estate had paid out more than $10,000 (approximately $300,000 today) for this purpose.

William Lee was at Mount Vernon when Martha Custis Washington died on May 22, 1802. He was there when the 153 people who had belonged to her dower share of her first husband's estate were divided up among her four grandchildren. He was there as this community of friends he'd lived with since he was sixteen years old also moved away.

William Lee was there when George Washington's heir, Bushrod Washington, moved in at Mount Vernon.

William Lee was there when Bushrod Washington moved his own enslaved people into the recently vacated slave quarters of the plantation.

As the years went by, William Lee saw many changes take place at Mount Vernon. The only thing that seemed to stay the same was the constant arrival of visitors. Lee still enjoyed seeing guests he knew from the days of the Revolutionary War. He may have recalled the dark days when it seemed America would lose the war—and how it felt to look across the battlefield to see the red coats of the enemy.

When a British diplomat visited Mount Vernon around 1805, he wrote that "there were about thirty Negroes belonging to the establishment at Mount Vernon, and an old mulatto servant who had served General Washington during the war in all his campaigns, and who inquired of me very earnestly after Lord Cornwallis."

No doubt Lee was curious about their old enemy twenty-five years after they defeated him. Lee was right behind General Washington as he commanded the victory over General Cornwallis at Yorktown, the last major battle of the war.

Visitors who had known Washington from the days of the Revolutionary War also knew William Lee. When artist Charles Willson Peale visited Mount Vernon in 1804 he wrote in his journal, "I inquired for the old Slave Servants of the General and was told they were all dead except William, his faithfull attendant through the war. I went to the Quarters (an out building so called) where I found him making shoes, he was now a cripple & in an extraordinary manner—both of his knee pans was moved from their places—was some inches higher up."

Lee's knees weren't his only problem during those years. He developed a serious drinking problem. He suffered from delirium tremens (DTs), which happens if someone who drinks a lot of alcohol goes through withdrawal when they stop. A young man named West Ford helped Lee when he was suffering and "frequently relieved him on such occasions, by bleeding him."

West Ford had been the property of George Washington's brother John Augustine Washington and his wife, Hannah Bushrod Washington. According to the terms of Hannah Washington's will, Ford was to be freed when he was twenty-one years old. When John Augustine and Hannah Washington's son, Bushrod Washington (who some historians believe may have been West Ford's father), inherited Mount Vernon after the death of Martha Washington, he moved West Ford with him to the plantation. Ford was freed about 1805, but he continued living and working at Mount Vernon.

In the winter of 1810, West Ford was called to help Lee again. But it was too late. William Lee was dead. He had lived and worked at Mount Vernon for more than forty years. He was likely buried in the slave cemetery, located about fifty yards from Washington's tomb.

CHRISTOPHER SHEELS

Christopher Sheels was one of the 153 enslaved people who were part of Martha Washington's dower estate and divided up between the four Custis grandchildren. (Sheels was inherited by G.W. P. Custis.) Twenty-seven-year-old Christopher Sheels had many different skills. He was a carpenter, house servant, and valet. Sheels' new master, began building a new home that overlooked the Potomac River and the new federal city, Washington, District of Columbia. Custis called his home Arlington House. Sheels would have served G.W.P. Custis at Arlington House.

It is unknown what happened to Christopher Sheels later in life.

ONEY JUDGE STAINES

George Washington died in 1799, just a few months after Oney Judge Staines and her daughter avoided capture in New Hampshire.

No one came looking for Oney Judge Staines after George Washington's death.

No one came looking for Oney Judge Staines after Martha Washington's death.

No one came looking for Oney Judge Staines ever again.

She lived as a free woman, even though the Custis estate still legally owned her. If she had returned to Mount Vernon years before, as the Washingtons wanted her to, Betsy Custis Law would have inherited her. Betsy Custis Law did inherit Oney Judge Staines' sister, Delphy Judge, and others, including Hercules' son, Richmond.

Oney Staines and her husband, Jack, settled down to live in Greenland, New Hampshire, when he returned from sea. In all, they had three children, Eliza, Nancy, and William. Jack died in 1803, leaving Oney Judge Staines a widow around the age of twenty-nine. She could not support herself and three children, so she moved in with the family of John and Phyllis Jack in Greenland, who had taken her in when she was hiding from Washington's nephew Burwell Bassett Jr. The two families banded together to survive.

Oney Judge Staines never remarried. All three of her children died when they were young adults, and none of them had children. Through the years, Oney Judge Staines and the two Jack daughters continued to live together. When the three women grew older they were very poor.

Of all the people owned by George or Martha Washington, only Oney Judge Staines left any sort of written recollections about her life's experience. She did not write them, but she consented to be interviewed by reporters twice when she was an elderly woman, once in May of 1845 and again in January of 1847.

Oney Judge Staines told the reporters that the Washingtons had never given her any sort of education or religious instruction. It was only after she arrived in Portsmouth that she learned to read and became a Christian. In an interview that appeared in the May 22, 1845, *Granite Freeman*, the reporter asked if she was "sorry she left Washington, as she had labored so much harder since." She answered, "No, I am free, and have, I trust, been made a child of God."

In the second interview, published in the abolitionist newspaper the *Liberator* on January 1, 1847, the reporter described Oney Judge Staines as being "nearly white, very much freckled." She was living with Nancy Jack, daughter of John and Phyllis Jack, in what he described as "an obscure place, and in a poor, cold house," and was being "maintained as a pauper" by Rockingham County, New Hampshire.

Oney Judge Staines died on February 25, 1848. She is buried in Greenland, New Hampshire.

HERCULES

Hercules ran away from Mount Vernon on Washington's birthday, February 22, 1797. He was never seen again.

At the time Hercules escaped, Richmond was twenty years old, Eve about fourteen, and Delia about twelve. When he left Mount Vernon, Hercules had no way to know that in about three years he would have been freed legally by the terms of Washington's will. But even then his three children would not have been freed. Their mother, Alice, was one of Martha Washington's "dower slaves," so all three of her children were too.

After Martha Washington's death, when her enslaved people were divided, Richmond, whose value was listed at £120, was inherited by Betsy Custis Law. Both of Hercules' daughters, Eve and Delia, were inherited by Nelly Custis Lewis and were moved to her nearby plantation, Woodlawn. Eve, who was described as a dwarf, was valued at £50. Delia was valued at £70.

PETER HARDIMAN

Peter Hardiman was one of the enslaved people rented by Washington. After the deaths of George and Martha Washington, G.W.P. Custis took Peter Hardiman with him to Arlington House, although the exact date isn't known.

Custis inherited Washington's prized donkey, Knight of Malta, which had been a gift from Lafayette. In 1844, G.W.P. Custis wrote an article that appeared in a book titled *The Gentleman's New Pocket Farrier, Comprising a General Description of the Noble and Useful Animal the Horse*. He described this animal as having "the fire and ferocity of a lion," and said he could "only be managed by one groom, and that always at considerable personal risk." That one groom was Peter Hardiman. In this article, Custis explained why he no longer had any jacks (male donkeys), writing, "Upon losing my groom (Peter) who was the first and last groom to the Mount Vernon Jacks, I parted with my stock."

It is not known exactly when Peter Hardiman died.

CAROLINE AND HER CHILDREN

Caroline, her husband Peter Hardiman, and their children were each inherited by G.W.P. Custis after the enslaved people who were part of Martha Washington's dower estate were divided. Caroline, with her skills as a seamstress and housemaid, was valued at £70 on the list of people who were inherited by Custis. It was far more than many other enslaved women.

Though it is not clear why, at some point later Caroline began using the name Caroline Branham or Brannum. After leaving Mount Vernon, Caroline had another child, a daughter named Lucy Harrison, born about 1806.

It is unclear what happened to Caroline later in life.

As for Caroline's children, specific details are known about what happened to some of them, while nothing is known about others.

Wilson, son of Caroline and Peter Hardiman

Seventeen-year-old Wilson went to work at Arlington House as groom in the stables with his father, Peter Hardiman. He was young and strong and given the value of £80.

Rachel, daughter of Caroline and Peter Hardiman

Rachel was about fifteen years old at the time of the division. She was valued at £50.

By 1813 Rachel had two daughters. Custis sold Rachel and her daughters with the understanding that their new owner would ultimately emancipate them. After Rachel was freed, she had two more children (both free because their mother was free).

Jemima, daughter of Caroline and Peter Hardiman

Jemima was about thirteen when G.W.P. Custis became her new master. Her value was listed at £40. It is unclear what happened to Jemima. However, slave manumission records in Alexandria list a woman named "Gemima Branham" who was freed in 1813 by her owner, Robert P. Washington. It is possible this was Jemima.

Leanthe, daughter of Caroline and Peter Hardiman

Leanthe was about eleven years old when their family left Mount Vernon. She was valued at £35. On October 11, 1820, William Costin, a free African American man, bought Leanthe and freed her six days later. Costin was the husband of Delphy Judge (Oney Judge's sister), whom he had purchased from Betsy Custis Law.

Polly, daughter of Caroline and Peter Hardiman

Polly was about nine years old when the "dower slaves" were divided up. She was valued at £30.

It is unknown what happened to Polly.

Peter, son of Caroline and Peter Hardiman

Peter was about seven years old at the time of the division. It is believed that young Peter was the person identified as "Branndum" on the list of those who were inherited by G.W.P. Custis. He was valued at £35.

It is unknown what happened to Peter.

Austin, son of Caroline and Peter Hardiman

Austin was born sometime before the death of Martha Washington. He was probably less than three years old when Martha Washington's heirs took possession of the enslaved people who were part of her dower estate. Austin was valued at £25.

He remained enslaved by G.W.P. Custis at Arlington House. Austin was still working at Arlington House when in 1831 Custis' daughter Mary married Robert E. Lee in the parlor.

As his stepgrandfather George Washington had done, G.W.P. Custis instructed in his will that the people be owned be freed. When he died in 1857, the executor of his will was his son-in-law, Robert E. Lee.

By the time all the paperwork was finalized, the Civil War was in full swing and Lee was a general in the Confederate army. On December 29, 1862, it was official: Sixty-five-year-old Austin Branham, the son of Martha Washington's housemaid Caroline, was free.

Daniel, son of Caroline and Peter Hardiman

Daniel was born sometime before the death of Martha Washington. He was probably younger than Austin, so he was likely about one year old when the division of the enslaved people occurred. He was valued at £20.

It is unknown what happened to Daniel.

Lucy Harrison, daughter of Caroline Branham

Lucy Harrison was born around 1806, about four years after her mother, Caroline, moved to Arlington House. Some historians believe George Washington Parke Custis may have

TOP: George Washington Parke (G.W.P.) Custis, Martha Washington's grandson, who grew up with the Washingtons at Mount Vernon, built Arlington House. Some of the enslaved people who came from Mount Vernon and served Custis at Arlington House were Christopher Sheels, and Caroline Branham and Peter Hardiman and all their children.

Custis' daughter, Mary, married Robert E. Lee, who became the famous Confederate general. During the Civil War, the union army took possession of Arlington House, then owned by the Lees. This photograph was taken on June 28, 1864, and show groups of men, some Union soldiers—including African Americans—at Arlington House. A couple of months later, the army began burying soldiers killed in the Civil War in Mrs. Lee's rose garden. This was the beginning of Arlington National Cemetery.

BOTTOM: Today Arlington House, built by G.W.P. Custis, sits within Arlington National Cemetery. This cemetery is an especially meaningful place as it is not only a burial ground, but also a shrine for veterans who have served the United States.

been Lucy's father. At some unknown point in time, G.W.P. Custis sold Lucy to a man named Robert H. Miller.

Lucy had two daughters named Sarah and Eugenia, and a son named Robert Henry Robinson. Eventually Lucy was emancipated along with an infant son named Charles. In the Alexandria County Free Negro Registers, 1797–1861, a note dated November 23, 1852, describes Lucy Ann Harrison as "a mulatto, about 44 years old, 5 feet 1 inch tall, of a copper color, with a mole on her left cheek. She was emancipated by R. H. Miller."

Miller, the man who owned Lucy and her children, sold her two daughters for $50 each—with the understanding that both Sarah and Eugenia would be freed when they turned twenty-one. The two girls took care of the children of their master, William Gregory. Their mistress taught Sarah and Eugenia to read. Later in life, the Gregory children recalled that Eugenia read stories to them, including "Ali Baba and the Forty Thieves." They also remembered Eugenia telling them Br'er Rabbit and the Tar Baby stories (African folktales long before they were published in American books). As promised, Sarah and Eugenia (Caroline Branham's granddaughters) were both freed when they turned twenty-one.

Lucy Harrison's son, Robert, was freed from slavery at some unknown time. He became a Methodist minister and was highly respected in the community. The Robert H. Robinson Library at the Alexandria Black History Museum is named in his honor.

Descendants of Caroline Branham, Lucy Harrison, and Robert Robinson live in the Washington, D.C., area. One of them, Zsun-nee Miller-Matema, worked as an interpreter at Mount Vernon, which ceased operating as a plantation in 1858 and is now a historic landmark. Zsun-nee guided visitors through the rooms of Mount Vernon that her ancestor Caroline cleaned more than two hundred years before.

This Windsor chair descended through the family of Caroline Branham and her daughter Lucy Harrison. After Lucy was emancipated, she lived as a free woman in Washington, D.C. In 1891, Lucy sold this chair to the Mount Vernon Ladies' Association. It is in their collection today.

Chapter Eight

Buried Lives

After George and Martha Washington died, visitors flocked to pay their respects at their tomb on the grounds of Mount Vernon. By 1831 the old tomb was in disrepair and a new one was built. The remains of the former president and first lady, along with other members of the Washington family, were moved to the new tomb.

Through the years visitors often wrote about the experience of viewing Washington's tomb. In November 1835, an anonymous article appeared in the *Alexandria Gazette* that was written by one such visitor. He had noticed eleven black men apparently cleaning up the area around the new tomb, and one woman who was cooking for them. When he asked who they were and what they were doing, the men explained that "they were a few of the many slaves freed by general George Washington, and they had offered their services upon this last and melancholy occasion, as the only return in their power to make to the remains of the man who had been more than a father to them; and they should continue their labors as long as any thing should be pointed out for them to do." The article reported that Nancy Quander was the woman who was cooking, and listed the names of the men: Sambo Anderson, William Anderson, Berkley Clark, William Hayes, Dick Jasper, Morris Jasper, George Lear, William Moss, Joe Richardson, Levi Richardson, and Joseph Smith. Not all of the men listed in the article had been owned by Washington; some were children of people he had owned during his lifetime.

One person George Washington had owned was Nancy Quander, the woman mentioned in the article. Nancy was about eleven years old when Washington died. She, her siblings, and her mother, Suckey Bay, who worked in the fields at River Farm, were freed by Washington's will.

Nancy later married a free black man named Charles Quander, a member of one of the oldest documented African American families in America. Many of the Quander family moved to nearby Gum Springs, a free black community founded by West Ford, who became the second wealthiest African American man in Fairfax County, Virginia. The Quander family became influential members of the community.

Some descendants of Nancy Quander still live in the area. In 1973, Gladys Quander Tancil, one of her descendants, became the first African American interpreter at Mount Vernon. Jay Quander formerly worked at Mount Vernon as the director of food and beverages. Another descendant, Rohulamin Quander, a retired senior administrative judge for the District of Columbia, serves as the family historian and works to keep alive the legacy of the Quander family.

Two other people mentioned in the 1835 newspaper article, Dick Jasper and his son Morris Jasper, also have descendants in the area. Phyllis Ford descended from Dick and Charity Jasper, both of whom had been owned by George Washington and worked in the fields. Ford's family line also stems from Morris Jasper, born to Dick and Charity Jasper after they were emancipated by Washington's will. Today Phyllis Ford is the President of Laurel Grove School Museum, a one-room schoolhouse opened in the 1880s and built on land deeded to it by William Jasper, the son of Morris Jasper (grandson of Dick and Charity Jasper). Former enslaved people in the area joined together to build a school where their children could be educated. Laurel Grove School is the last remaining one-room schoolhouse still in existence that was once part of the Fairfax County segregated school system. It opened as a museum in 2004.

~

Most visitors to Washington's tomb through the years were unaware that Mount Vernon's slave cemetery was only about fifty yards away. But one day in 1845, another anonymous visitor's story about his chance encounter there appeared in a publication called the *Western Literary Messenger*. His visit took place when John Augustine Washington III was the owner of Mount Vernon.

While standing at George Washington's tomb, the man noticed a few people working a short distance away. He walked over to see what they were doing. He recorded that "they were enclosing with a paling [a small fence made of stakes or pickets] a grave very neatly sodded, and some sweet briar was still clinging to its native turf upon it. It was the grave of a favorite servant, an aged colored woman, whose good and amiable character had won respect and regard.—'When did she die?' we enquired. 'She parted from us last Sunday,' was the reply." The visitor's account continued: "There are many graves in the grove, and one of the servants pointed out that of Washington's favorite servant, who was with him in his campaigns, fulfilling his simple duties faithfully and affectionately. The spot is not forgotten, though the tramp of passing years has leveled the little mound. Nor was the humble cemetery a mournful spot: the birds were singing merrily in the trees, and the hand of Spring was molding the wild flower, and training vines over the graves."

Today such details recorded by visitors to Mount Vernon are historic treasures that allow us to hear conversations from long ago. But at the time, the owners of Mount Vernon considered the visitors to be a nuisance. While George and Martha Washington were alive, they understood their public role and accepted the constant stream of guests to their home. But the relatives of George Washington who later inherited Mount Vernon were not public figures.

After George Washington's death, Martha Washington owned his estate for the rest of her life. After her death, two and a half years after her husband's, Mount Vernon's next owner was Bushrod Washington, George Washington's nephew.

When Bushrod Washington died, he left Mount Vernon to his nephew John Augustine Washington II.

When John Augustine Washington II died, he left Mount Vernon to his son, John Augustine Washington III.

None of those men wanted crowds of uninvited people to swarm all over the estate. Yet visitors barged onto their private property at will. Curious strangers asked to see inside the mansion house. So many people picked flowers from the garden that the family had to post signs telling them not to. Though its owners didn't wish for it to happen, Mount Vernon slowly became an unofficial tourist destination and national landmark.

Another slow change was happening around the estate. George Washington's heirs did not maintain the house and grounds of Mount Vernon as meticulously as he had—and it showed. By the 1850s John Augustine Washington III wanted Mount Vernon, its finances, and its visitors off his hands, and asked both the federal government and the state of Virginia to purchase Mount Vernon. Neither would.

Then a woman floated by who changed everything.

In the fall of 1853, Louisa Bird Cunningham, a wealthy woman from South Carolina, was traveling down the Potomac River on a steamboat. It was naval custom that ships passing by the tomb of George Washington at Mount Vernon would ring their bells to honor America's first commander in chief. On the night the ship was to pass by Mount

Vernon, Cunningham listened for the expected bell. When she heard it she made her way to the deck to see Washington's home.

As the ship chugged by in the darkness, Cunningham looked toward the Virginia shore with anticipation. The house that had been so dearly loved by George Washington sat on top of the hill. Moonlight fell on Mount Vernon and illuminated the massive two-story piazza that faced the river.

It was sagging.

The whole house looked shabby and dilapidated.

Cunningham was shocked. Washington had been gone for just over fifty years, and his house was so badly deteriorated that it looked as if it would soon be gone too.

Cunningham wrote a letter describing the sight to her daughter, thirty-seven-year-old Ann Pamela Cunningham. "I was painfully distressed at the ruin and desolation of the home of Washington and the thought passed through my mind: Why was it that the women of his country did not try to keep it in repair, if the men could not do it? It does seem such a blot on our country!"

Ann Pamela Cunningham took hold of the idea. She founded the Mount Vernon Ladies' Association (MVLA) and challenged the women of America to raise money to buy the home. It was a monumental task. But they succeeded. In 1858, John Augustine Washington III agreed to sell the MVLA the house and two hundred acres for $200,000.

~

According to the 1860 census, the total population of black and biracial people in America at that time numbered 4,441,830. Of that number, 3,953,760 were held in slavery. When these numbers are compared to the first national census, of 1790, when Washington was president, it is clear that the total population of enslaved people had grown significantly.

The 1790 census records the total number of enslaved people within the United States and its territories as 697,697. (According to that census, Washington's home state of Virginia had 292,627—more than 40 percent of all the enslaved people in the country.) Using these census figures, the population of men, women, and children bound in slavery in America had grown more than five and a

TOP: This 1858 photograph shows the deterioration of Mount Vernon as well as some of the changes Washington's heirs made to the house through the years. Notice several ship masts have been used to help support the roof of the porch.

BOTTOM: Mount Vernon today. The Mount Vernon Ladies' Association owns and operates George Washington's home without federal funds. Each year about one million visitors arrive to see Washington's home and pay their respects at his tomb.

half times in the seventy years between 1790 and 1860.

About three years after the MVLA took possession of Mount Vernon, and a year after the 1860 census was conducted, the Civil War began. Since the plantation was the home of George Washington, both North and South agreed that Mount Vernon would be a neutral zone. It was also physically situated between the two sides' capitals, with the Union capital in Washington, D.C., and the Confederate capital in Richmond, Virginia.

The Civil War lasted four long, bloody years.

West Ford, the man who tried to help William Lee during his last days, was a free man but still living at Mount Vernon during the early years of the war. He died in 1863. Some believe Ford might be the last person buried in the slave cemetery at Mount Vernon.

Until the Mount Vernon Ladies' Association bought Mount Vernon, various members of the Washington family had owned it, and generation after generation of enslaved people had lived, worked, died, and been buried there.

The Civil War brought an end to slavery in America.

Never again would a baby be born into slavery at Mount Vernon.

Never again would an enslaved man, woman, or child be buried there.

After slavery was abolished, most of those who had lived in servitude at Mount Vernon moved away. But a few stayed and became paid employees of the Mount Vernon Ladies' Association.

~

Back in 1845, the location of the grave of "Washington's favorite servant" was pointed out to a Mount Vernon visitor. That same year, the grave of the dearly loved elderly woman who had a "good and amiable" character was marked. But eventually, no one was left at Mount Vernon who knew where William Lee or the good old woman were buried.

Ultimately no one was left anywhere who knew the location of *any* grave at Mount Vernon—or the names of the people who rested there.

Year after year following Washington's death, the summer sun had warmed the cemetery's narrow strip of land where his enslaved people were buried. Rain fell. Leaves of red and gold drifted to the ground. Hail bounced. Snow drifted into piles, melted, and made way for spring.

Washington's tomb, tended and maintained, remained the same. In the slave cemetery the weeds and underbrush grew in a tangle over the unmarked graves beneath a canopy of hardwood trees. When visitors to Washington's tomb had walked to the small bit of land overlooking the Potomac River, they would not have known it was a burial ground. There were no signs. No headstones. No indication at all that many lives lay buried below their feet. In life, these men, women, and children were anonymous even as they played an instrumental role in the history of Mount Vernon, George Washington's life, and the founding of America. In death they were anonymous because no one knew who they were or where they were laid to rest.

In 1928, the Mount Vernon Ladies' Association realized there was almost no trace of the cemetery. They understood that the very memory of its location was in danger of being lost. To make sure that didn't happen, the MVLA had a marker created that said:

This marker placed by the Mount Vernon Ladies' Association in 1929 is still in the cemetery today.

IN MEMORY
OF THE
MANY FAITHFUL
COLORED SERVANTS
OF THE
WASHINGTON FAMILY
BURIED AT
MOUNT VERNON
FROM
1760 TO 1860
THEIR
UNIDENTIFIED GRAVES
SURROUND THIS SPOT
1929

That marker, placed in the slave cemetery in 1929 (which uses an outdated term to describe African Americans), is believed by the MVLA to be the first of its kind at a historic plantation.

But as the decades passed, weeds and underbrush grew once more, now in a tangle over the 1929 memorial stone as well as the graves. Once again, when visitors to Washington's tomb had walked to the narrow strip of land overlooking the Potomac River, they would not have known it was a burial ground.

Then, in 1982, a reporter named Dorothy Gilliam visited Mount Vernon. On February 2 of that year, Gilliam's article titled "Remembrance" appeared in the *Washington Post*. In it

LEFT: This arched brick gate marks the entrance to the cemetery of the enslaved people of Mount Vernon.

RIGHT: The memorial monument honors the enslaved people buried in the cemetery whose graves are unmarked.

she wrote that she walked "the path the slaves trod to bury their kin. I walked upon the surprisingly still red leaves that formed an incongruously colorful canopy atop the nameless bodies underneath." In the cemetery she found the overgrown 1929 memorial that had been there more than fifty years. Gilliam closed her article with the words "And no one seems to have thought much about it since."

By fall of that year, the MVLA had plans to build a new memorial that would commemorate the cemetery. The winner of a design competition sponsored by the Howard University School of Architecture and Planning and the National Association for the Advancement of Colored People would determine the look of the memorial.

The memorial, erected in 1983, begins at a brick archway at the entrance of the cemetery. A path leads visitors to three circles upon which are inscribed the words "faith," "hope," and "love." In the center stands a truncated gray granite column that reads:

IN MEMORY OF
THE AFRO AMERICANS
WHO SERVED AS SLAVES
AT MOUNT VERNON
THIS MONUMENT
MARKING THEIR
BURIAL GROUND
DEDICATED

SEPTEMBER 21, 1983
MOUNT VERNON
LADIES' ASSOCIATION

For the first time, the public had a place to pay their respects to the enslaved people of Mount Vernon who are buried there.

But still, the names of individuals interred there were lost to time. Even the locations of graves in the cemetery were unknown.

~

In 1985, Mount Vernon hoped to learn more about the number of graves and their locations. They conducted a geophysical survey (information gathered on what is below the surface) using ground-penetrating radar (GPR). The survey found sixty-six readings that might have indicated graves. But the GPR could not determine the locations of any grave shafts for certain.

Seven years after the 1983 memorial at the cemetery site was dedicated, Sheila Coates, founder and president of Black Women United for Action (BWUFA), believed more should be done to focus on the members of the enslaved community who lived, worked, and died at Mount Vernon. In 1990 Mount Vernon and BWUFA held a commemoration ceremony. In an article in the *Washington Post* on September 23, 1990, Coates is quoted as saying, "This is not about slavery, it's about the strength of the people who endured slavery."

Every year since 1990, Mount Vernon and BWUFA have hosted a remembrance ceremony. In 1998, fifteen years after the unveiling of the memorial at Mount Vernon's slave cemetery, the General Assembly of Virginia recognized the efforts of BWUFA with a commendation crediting the organization for "focusing attention on the Slave Memorial at Mount Vernon and on the many contributions to the formation of this nation made by the unknown slaves buried there."

In 1994, in order to protect visitors to the cemetery from getting too close to the edge of the hill, Mount Vernon planned to build a fence. Dr. Esther White, who was then Mount Vernon's director of archaeology, excavated small test pits to ensure fence postholes would not disturb any historic archaeological evidence. It was the first archaeological work ever done on the cemetery site. Dr. White saw that the soil color in the test pits suggested the presence of graves. To confirm it, the team continued to remove the top layer of soil. Dr. White "realized the cemetery's grave shafts were amazingly clear, visible just a few inches below the current ground surface." In order not to disturb any graves, a stacked rail fence that did not require postholes was built.

Dr. White never forgot how clearly recognizable the grave shafts were. She understood how much information could be gained through a full-scale archaeological dig, and hoped one day it would happen.

Starting around 2013, projects at Mount

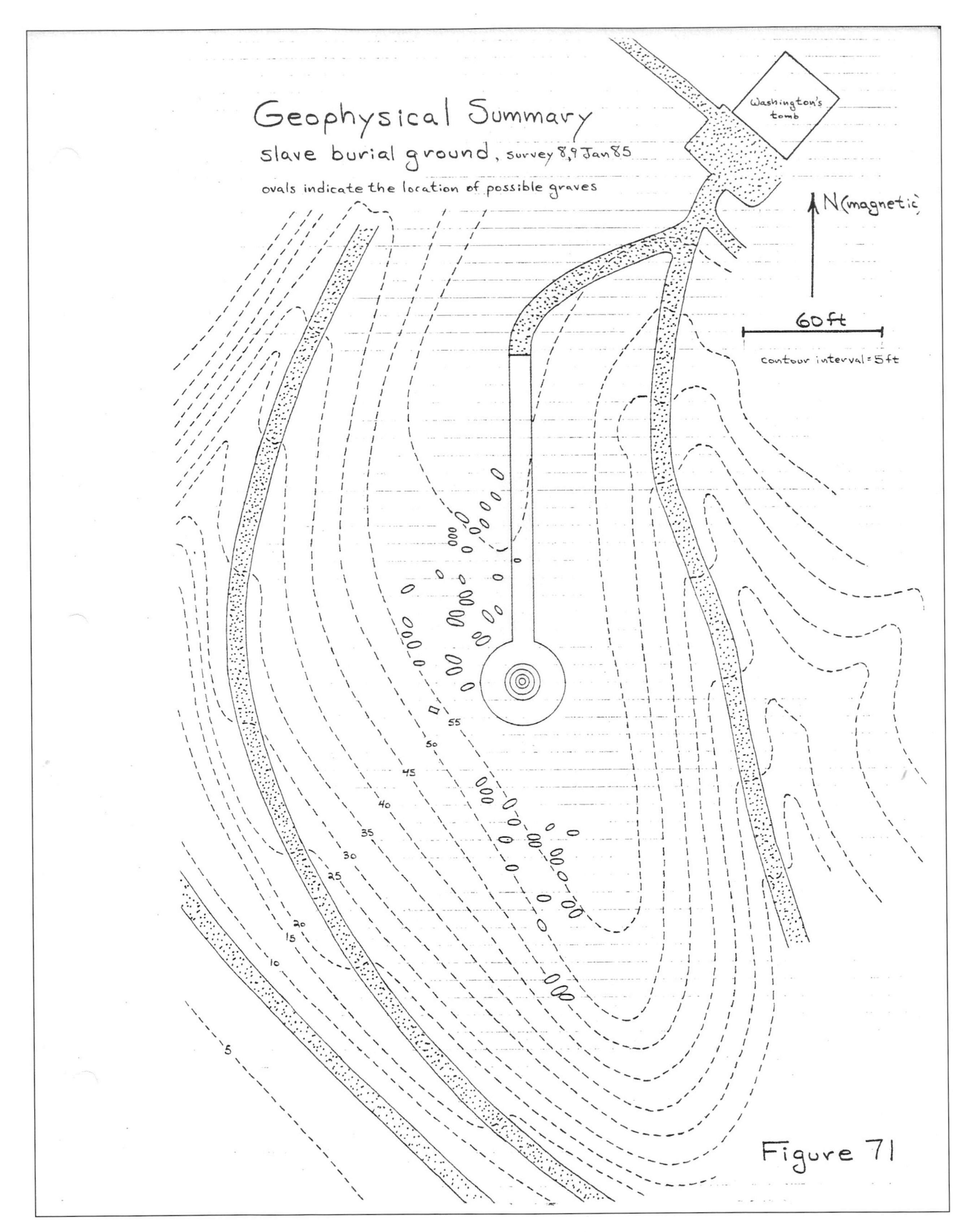

The 1985 geophysical survey shows possible locations of graves.

Vernon began that would expand the knowledge of the enslaved community that worked there. Molly Kerr, digital humanities program manager, developed a database to record facts about individual enslaved men, women, and children. By searching through historic documents, Kerr and her team identified six hundred individuals by name and recorded details about each person. The scholarship of this database allows researchers to follow specific events in the lives of individual people as never before.

By 2014, the hopes of Dr. White and the team of archaeologists at Mount Vernon were becoming a reality. An archaeological study of the cemetery site would move forward at last. The archaeologists' goal was to answer three questions:

- Where are the cemetery's boundaries?
- How many people are buried there?
- How are burials arranged within the cemetery?

Because the site is a sacred burial ground, archaeologists Dr. White, who by then was the director of historic preservation, and Dr. Eleanor Breen, who had been named the deputy director of archaeology, held a public informational meeting before the work began. Members of the community and BWUFA were in attendance. Dr. Breen described the project as a multi-year archaeological dig of the cemetery site where some of Mount Vernon's enslaved people were buried.

Dr. Breen explained that no human remains would be disturbed during the dig, and told attendees, "We may never know the names of the individuals who are buried here, but we want to be sure that they go 'unnumbered' no longer."

~

On May 15, 2014, a few dozen visitors made their way toward the slave cemetery. The group included Mount Vernon staff members, people from the community, and some descendants of people who were once owned by the Washingtons and worked at Mount Vernon. They came together on a perfect spring day for a Blessing Ceremony that would launch the archaeological survey of the

Archaeology meets modern technology as a drone takes aerial images of the cemetery area.

cemetery. Sheila Coates believes the project will allow the enslaved people who are buried there to be "recognized for the sacrifices they gave." Under the trees and over the unmarked graves they gathered to pray, sing, and remember.

Curt Viebranz, then the president of Mount Vernon, said, "We seek to commemorate the lives of those free and enslaved individuals who lived and died here at Mount Vernon by thoroughly documenting the locations of individual burial plots."

Rev. Dr. Darrell Keith White, pastor of Bethlehem Baptist Church in Gum Springs, spoke about the "unnumbered trailblazers who rest beneath this hallowed space." Larry King sang "Amazing Grace." Dean Norton played "Taps." Finally, soil from each of Washington's five farms was mixed together and sprinkled on a commemorative wreath.

Mount Vernon's archaeologists began the project that will investigate 55,000 square feet of the area. It will take several years to complete. The dig season runs from about June through October. At the end of each dig season the graves that have been uncovered and documented are re-covered.

Following the usual practice of an archaeological dig, they began with a survey of the area and mapped out a grid pattern. Each square in the grid is five feet by five feet. To begin the work in a square, archaeologists carefully remove leaves and the top layer of soil.

As soil is removed, it is placed on a screen that has quarter-inch holes. Dirt falls through the screen, but any possible artifacts stay on top. They are collected and labeled so archaeologists will know exactly where they came from. Back in the lab, any material collected is cleaned and studied carefully. Layer by layer, soil within the square is removed and examined for artifacts. Only the top six to eight inches of soil is removed. This is deep enough to reveal the presence of a grave shaft, but not deep enough to disturb remains buried there.

Once the archaeologists have removed the upper layers of soil within a square, they can see any color variations that might exist. Graves are easy to spot once the topsoil is removed. Why? The soil of a grave is a different color than the surrounding soil. It also has an oval shape, and it is about six

TOP: Both Eleanor Mudd and Dave Rensch have volunteered to work at the archaeological dig every season. In this photo they are using a sifting screen. All of the excavated soil is poured through the screen to separate the soil from any possible artifacts. Any material of interest they find is bagged and labeled, which tells the archaeologists where the objects were found.

BOTTOM: In the lab, volunteer workers (left to right) Patricia Kristoff, Francois Krodel, Stephanie Will, and Linda Flint wash, label, and identify the contents of each bag. Even though most objects look like rocks, each piece is cleaned and examined to see if it is a historical artifact.

This yellowish oval shape is a grave shaft. The color is different because soil that is dug out and then replaced will look different from the undisturbed soil around it.

feet long. Why is the soil a different color? When someone digs a grave, the soil from the shaft being dug is tossed aside on the ground. When the soil is returned to the grave shaft to fill it in, it is the same dirt, but it is jumbled up and mixed with leaves and grass. That soil has been forever changed and will always look different from the undisturbed soil around it.

If a grave is found in one of the squares, the archaeologists remove the topsoil in the next square. One by one, graves are located and their locations documented. The human remains below are never disturbed.

As their work progresses, the archaeologists at Mount Vernon compare the 1985 geophysical survey readings to the evidence from the dig. So far about 82 percent of the GPR readings thought to indicate graves have proved to be correct. Some areas that were thought to be graves were not graves after all. And the GPR completely missed some actual grave locations.

In their work at Mount Vernon, archaeologists have found evidence of another group of people whose lives have often been forgotten. Native Americans were present on this site long before the Washington family

Joe Downer, crew chief for the project, cleans off one of the graves—the final resting place for a child. Since many babies and children did not survive to adulthood during the eighteenth century, archaeologists have discovered many child-sized graves.

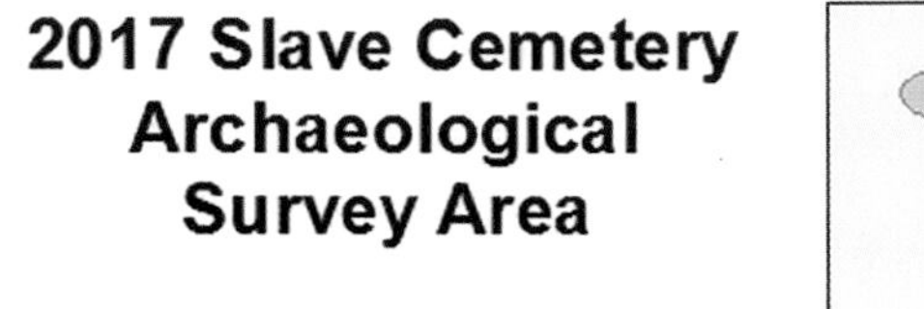

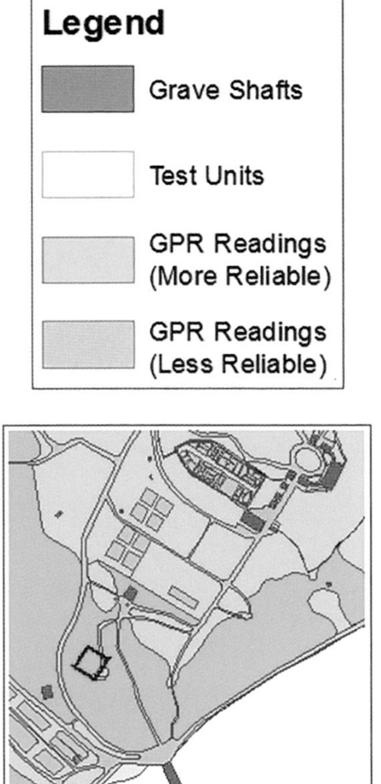

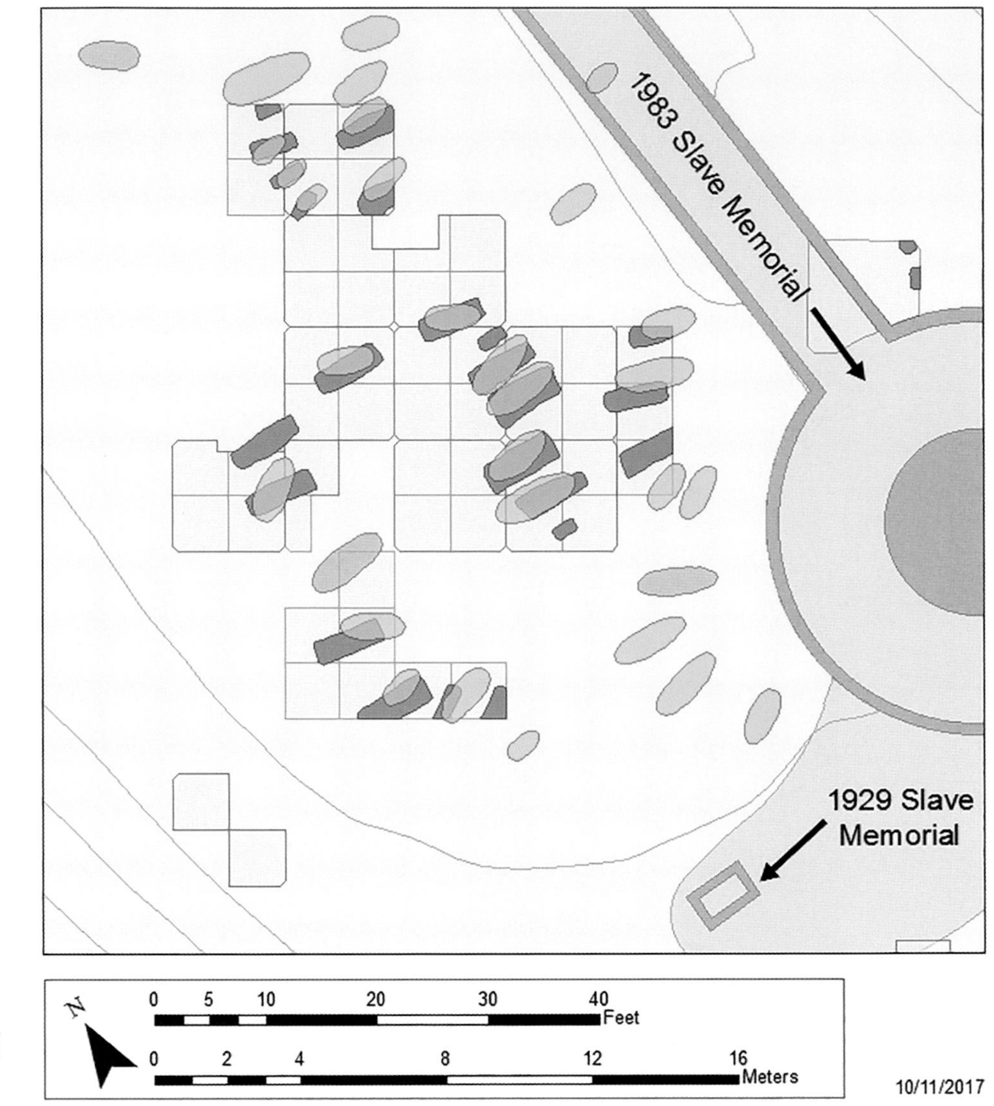

This map of the area shows the ground-penetrating radar (GPR) results as well as the archaeological results as of 2017. The blue places indicate actual grave shafts. The archaeologists expect to find more graves as the dig continues.

arrived and designated it a burial ground for the people enslaved at their plantation. Many prehistoric arrowheads have been uncovered there, and countless tiny slivers of stone indicate Native Americans used the location as a work site to make stone tools.

Very few artifacts have been found on the cemetery site that may have belonged to the Washingtons' enslaved people, but archaeologists have uncovered one piece that was a highly personal item. It is a glass button with a coral motif that was originally set in brass. It is similar to a button found at the site of the slave quarters. Since both buttons were found in areas used by the enslaved people, the archaeologists speculate that they may have been a set of cuff links. It is impossible to know for certain.

These glass buttons with coral motifs may have been part of a set of cuff links. The one on the left was found in the cemetery; the other was found during an archaeological dig in the House for Families living quarters.

Archaeology makes it possible to find artifacts not only in the cemetery but also in other parts of Mount Vernon. Dr. Breen says, "Visible, tangible, and buried in the ground are the footings of the homes of enslaved people, the broken plates from which they ate their meals, the objects that gave their lives meaning, and the ways in which they buried their loved ones." These physical pieces of history provide insight into the daily lives of those who were enslaved by giving us a glimpse of details such as the patterns on the dishes they used.

~

When the first field season of the archaeological dig was over in the fall of 2014, Mount Vernon and Black Women United for Action hosted the annual remembrance ceremony to honor the people who were enslaved at Mount Vernon. When attendees arrived at the cemetery site they could see rows of graves that had been revealed during the dig. Each oval in the soil was the final resting place of an individual who lived and died at the plantation. A bouquet of fresh flowers lay on each grave. For the first time in centuries the site felt like a cemetery. The presence of the flower-topped graves made the remembrance ceremony deeply meaningful. It seemed to Sheila Coates that the "tentacles of slavery are reaching from the earth. The whole project brought to life those enslaved at Mount Vernon." Dr. White saw that "the power of archaeology completely transformed a wooded lot into something sacred and visible, a tangible reminder of the people who were enslaved at the plantation."

Each year during the dig season, visitors to the cemetery are welcome to watch the archaeologists at work and ask questions. The archaeologists at Mount Vernon who lead the dig in the cemetery understand the importance of their work. Joe Downer, crew chief of the archaeological dig, says, "It is a profound thing to uncover and identify a grave shaft. Each outline that we see represents a single individual, someone who lived, forged relationships, made memories, and had both joy-filled and sorrowful life experiences that helped shape who they were. The fact that many of these individuals were forced to live in a system that denied them their humanity makes their story all the more powerful. I think it is compelling for visitors to see these grave sites because it forces them to think of the enslaved individual, and the enslaved community, in a way that is not possible on other areas of the estate."

Luke Pecoraro, director of archaeology, says the work "is a direct tangible link to the enslaved community over multiple generations." He understands that the excavation can be an emotional place for visitors and that it enables the archaeologists "to connect with people about the history of Mount Vernon and its past as linked to slavery." Pecoraro sees "the impact that archaeological fieldwork and research can have to make a visit more meaningful."

This archaeological dig isn't just for the experts. Volunteers are welcome and encouraged to help with the work. On average 83 people volunteer in the cemetery each year. Of this number, some work once or twice but about ten different people work there on a regular basis. Joe Downer says, "History belongs to all of us, and the story of slavery in this country is no different. Having volunteers take part in this project allows our nation's diverse communities to come together to honor the lives of those that made it all possible."

As part of my research for writing this book, I participated in the cemetery archaeological dig. I met up with the team in the cool of the morning, long before visitors entered the gates to see George Washington's Mount Vernon. We loaded the tools needed for the day into a motorized utility vehicle. Gear included high-tech equipment like the Total Station (a precision laser used to determine the exact location of each grave site) and low-tech tools like bug spray, gloves, and shovels. Next aboard the vehicle were the archaeologists and the team of volunteers. Some of the volunteers have worked on the dig every day since it began. It is physically demanding, but they give their time and energy to honor those who are buried in the cemetery.

When the crew and I arrived at the cemetery, it felt peaceful. Birds were singing and a slow breeze was blowing through the treetops. The experienced team immediately got to work. The first step was to take off the tarp that covered the dig site. Rainwater that had pooled in small puddles on the tarp was scooped out. When the tarp was removed, I caught the earthy scent of leaves and soil.

Although I'd seen photos of the grave shafts, this was the first time I saw them with my own eyes. Dappled sunlight shone down on several graves clearly outlined in the Virginia soil. I stared at them. Even though I could hear the sound of a jet flying overhead, hundreds of years seemed to melt away and I could imagine all the people I'd come to know through my research and written about: William Lee, Christopher Sheels, Caroline, Peter Hardiman, Oney Judge, Hercules. Each of them had probably buried a loved one here and heard birds singing or wind rustling the treetops nearby. Maybe they had once stood in the same spot where I was standing.

The archaeological team went to work on the next five-by-five-foot square. Three-fourths of a grave shaft had already been uncovered in the square beside this one, and we would be uncovering the remainder of the shaft. This was the sixty-seventh grave to be found and documented.

As layers of soil were shoveled out, we sifted it to separate dirt from possible artifacts. Anything of interest was placed in a labeled bag. Items unearthed that day included a five-thousand-year-old arrowhead, a small shard of Native American pottery, and many stone flakes from the creation of stone tools centuries ago. At each level, the archaeologist determined exact positions with the Total Station laser, made notes about the color and texture of the soil, and collected dirt samples.

I took a turn doing as many parts of the dig as possible. That included using a trowel to remove the soil from the top of the grave shaft. Even though the shaft had been dug more than two hundred years before, I could tell the soil that had long ago backfilled the grave was different from the soil surrounding it. On my knees with the trowel, I scraped away layers of dirt. I would never know the identity of the individual who lay in the grave beneath me. Whoever rested at the bottom of grave No. 67 had likely been enslaved their entire life. What sort of work had they done at Mount Vernon? While doing my research had I seen their name mentioned in a letter or on a farm report? Was this the grave of William Lee?

By the end of the workday, about eight inches of soil had been removed from the grid section. The entire grave shaft was exposed for the first time since it was dug.

~

The work of the archaeological dig continues each year. As of this writing, the locations

of seventy graves have been found. Twenty-three are graves of children and forty-seven are graves of adults. Each year the dig will reveal the locations of more graves.

At the conclusion of each field season, when Mount Vernon and Black Women United for Action host a remembrance ceremony, the graves that were located and documented during the season are covered up once more.

But those final resting places of the enslaved men, women, and children who lived, worked, and are buried at Mount Vernon are no longer forgotten.

LEFT and ABOVE: Flowers adorn these graves of enslaved men, women, and children who lived, worked, and died at Mount Vernon. William Lee is likely buried in this cemetery, and it is possible his brother, Frank Lee, and Hercules' wife, Alice, are too. Without death and burial records, it is impossible to know for certain where anyone specific is buried, or the names of the individuals who lie in each grave. But now, after hundreds of years, the locations of many of these final resting places have been found—and will not be forgotten.

Washington's Own Words About Slavery

1761

Fairfax County (*Virginia*) *Auguſt* 11, 1761.

RAN away from a Plantation of the Subſcriber's, on *Dogue-Run* in *Fairfax*, on Sunday the 9th Inſtant, the following Negroes, *viz.*

Peros, 35 or 40 Years of Age, a well-ſet Fellow, of about 5 Feet 8 Inches high, yellowiſh Complexion, with a very full round Face, and full black Beard, his Speech is ſomething ſlow and broken, but not in ſo great a Degree as to render him remarkable. He had on when he went away, a dark colour'd Cloth Coat, a white Linen Waiſtcoat, white Breeches and white Stockings.

Jack, 30 Years (or thereabouts) old, a ſlim, black, well made Fellow, of near 6 Feet high, a ſmall Face, with Cuts down each Cheek, being his Country Marks, his Feet are large (or long) for he requires a great Shoe: The Cloathing he went off in cannot be well aſcertained, but it is thought in his common working Dreſs, ſuch as Cotton Waiſtcoat (of which he had a new One) and Breeches, and Oſnabrig Shirt.

Neptune, aged 25 or 30, well-ſet, and of about 5 Feet 8 or 9 Inches high, thin jaw'd, his Teeth ſtragling and fil'd ſharp, his Back, if rightly remember'd, has many ſmall Marks or Dots running from both Shoulders down to his Waiſtband, and his Head was cloſe ſhaved: Had on a Cotton Waiſtcoat, black or dark colour'd Breeches, and an Oſnabrig Shirt.

Cupid, 23 or 25 Years old, a black well made Fellow, 5 Feet 8 or 9 Inches high, round and full faced, with broad Teeth before, the Skin of his Face is coarſe, and inclined to be pimpley, he has no other diſtinguiſhable Mark that can be recollected; he carried with him his common working Cloaths, and an old Oſnabrigs Coat made Frockwiſe.

The two laſt of theſe Negroes were bought from an *African* Ship in *Auguſt* 1759, and talk very broken and unintelligible *Engliſh*; the ſecond one, *Jack*, is Countryman to thoſe, and ſpeaks pretty good *Engliſh*, having been ſeveral Years in the Country. The other, *Peros*, ſpeaks much better than either, indeed has little of his Country Dialect left, and is eſteemed a ſenſible judicious Negro.

As they went off without the leaſt Suſpicion, Provocation, or Difference with any Body, or the leaſt angry Word or Abuſe from their Overſeers, 'tis ſuppoſed they will hardly lurk about in the Neighbourhood, but ſteer ſome direct Courſe (which cannot even be gueſſed at) in Hopes of an Eſcape: Or, perhaps, as the Negro *Peros* has lived many Years about *Williamſburg*, and *King-William* County, and *Jack* in *Middleſex*, they may poſſibly bend their Courſe to one of thoſe Places.

Whoever apprehends the ſaid Negroes, ſo that the Subſcriber may readily get them, ſhall have, if taken up in this County, Forty Shillings Reward, beſide what the Law allows; and if at any greater Diſtance, or out of the Colony, a proportionable Recompence paid them, by

GEORGE WASHINGTON.

N. B. If they ſhould be taken ſeparately, the Reward will be proportioned.

On August 11, 1761, George Washington posted this ad for four runaways. It is believed that all four of the enslaved people mentioned were returned to Mount Vernon.

1766

"With this Letter comes a Negro (Tom) which I beg the favour of you to sell, in any of the Islands you may go to, for whatever he will fetch ... this Fellow is both a Rogue & Runaway ... he is exceeding healthy, strong, and good at the Hoe ... he may, with your good management, sell well, if kept clean & trim'd up a little when offerd to Sale ... and must beg the favour of you (least he shoud attempt his escape) to keep him handcuffd till you get to Sea—or in the Bay."

July 2, 1766, George Washington to Joseph Thompson, a sea captain sailing to the West Indies

1774

ARTICLE 17 OF THE FAIRFAX RESOLVES:
Resolved that it is the Opinion of this Meeting, that during our present Difficulties and Distress, no Slaves ought to be imported into any of the British Colonies on this Continent; and we take this Opportunity of declaring our most earnest Wishes to see an entire Stop for ever put to such a wicked cruel and unnatural Trade.

July 18, 1774, George Washington signed the Fairfax Resolves. He was the chairman of the committee in Virginia that wrote the document.

~ 1778 ~

"For this Land also I had rather give Negroes—if Negroes would do. for to be plain I wish to get quit of Negroes."

August 15, 1778, George Washington
to Lund Washington, his farm manager

~ 1779 ~

"My scruples arise from a reluctance in offering these people at public vendue, and on account of the uncertainty of timeing the sale well—In the first case, if these poor wretches are to be held in a state of slavery, I do not see that a change of masters will render it more irksome, provided husband & wife, and Parents & children are not separated from each other, which is not my intention to do."

February 24–26, 1779, George Washington
to Lund Washington

~ 1786 ~

"I hope it will not be conceived from these observations, that it is my wish to hold the unhappy people who are the subject of this letter, in slavery. I can only say that there is not a man living who wishes more sincerely than I do, to see a plan adopted for the abolition of it—but there is only one proper and effectual mode by which it can be accomplished, & that is by Legislative authority."

April 12, 1786, George Washington
to Robert Morris

"The benevolence of your heart my Dr Marqs is so conspicuous upon all occasions, that I never wonder at any fresh proofs of it; but your late purchase of an Estate in the Colony of Cayenne with a view of emancipating the slaves on it, is a generous and noble proof of your humanity. Would to God a like spirit would diffuse itself generally into the minds of the people of this country, but I despair of seeing it—some petitions were presented to the Assembly at its last Session, for the abolition of slavery, but they could scarcely obtain a reading. To set them afloat at once would, I really believe, be productive of much inconvenience & mischief; but by degrees it certainly might, & assuredly ought to be effected & that too by Legislative authority."

May 10, 1786, George Washington
to the Marquis de Lafayette

"I never mean (unless some particular circumstances should compel me to it) to possess another slave by purchase; it being among my first wishes to see some plan adopted, by the legislature by which slavery in this Country may be abolished by slow, sure, & imperceptable degrees."

September 9, 1786, George Washington
to John Mercer

"With respect to the negroes, I conclude it is not in my power to answer your wishes—because it is as much against my own inclination as it can be against your's, to hurt the feelings of those unhappy people by a separation of man and wife, or of families."

November 24, 1786, George Washington to John Mercer

~ 1794 ~

"With respect to the other species of property, concerning which you ask my opinion, I shall frankly declare to you that I do not like even to think much less talk of it. However, as you have put the question, I shall, in a few words, give you my ideas of it. Were it not then, that I am principled agt selling Negroes, as you would Cattle in the market, I would not, in twelve months from this date, be possessed of one as a slave."

November 23, 1794, George Washington to Alexander Spotswood

~ 1797 ~

"I wish from my Soul that the Legislature of this State could see the policy of a gradual abolition of Slavery."

August 4, 1797, George Washington to Lawrence Lewis

~ 1798 ~

"Slaves were bequeathed to us by Europeans, and time alone can change them; an event, sir, which you may believe me, no man desires more heartily than I do. Not only do I pray for it, on the score of human dignity, but I can clearly foresee that nothing but the rooting out of slavery can perpetuate the existence of our union, by consolidating it in a common bond of principle."

Summer 1798, John Bernard's account of his conversation with George Washington

~ 1799 ~

"It is demonstratively clear, that on this Estate [Mount Vernon] I have more working Negros by a full moiety [half] than can be employed to any advantage in the farming System; and I shall never turn Planter thereon.

"To sell the overplus I cannot, because I am principled against this kind of traffic in the human species. To hire them out, is almost as bad, because they could not be disposed of in families to any advantage, and to disperse the families I have an aversion."

August 17, 1799, George Washington to Robert Lewis

"The unfortunate condition of the persons, whose labour in part I employed, has been the only unavoidable subject of regret."

Unknown date sometime toward the end of Washington's life, recorded by his friend and biographer David Humphreys.

Source Notes

(For complete citation information for Founders Online sources, see Selected Bibliography.)

INTRODUCTION

p.1. The majority (approximately 95 percent) . . . in Africa. "Estimates," Voyages: The Trans-Atlantic Slave Trade Database.

p.5. "among my first wishes . . . imperceptable degrees." George Washington to John Francis Mercer, 9 September 1786, *Founders Online.*

p.5. "The unfortunate condition . . . unavoidable subject of regret." Humphreys, 78.

CHAPTER ONE / William Lee

p.10 Enslaved children got fewer clothes than the adults. Mary V. Thompson, "The Only Unavoidable Subject of Regret": George Washington, Slavery, and the Enslaved Community at Mount Vernon (Pending publication 2019, University of Virginia Press), 217.

p.10. With his horn on his back . . . through the tangled woods. Custis, 387.

p.12. "saw [General Washington] and his colored servant . . . talking to them." Dann, 408–409.

p.12. "If it will give Will any pleasure . . . are both very well." Thompson, Mary V. "William Lee & Oney Judge: A Look at George Washington & Slavery." *Journal of the American Revolution,* 28 Aug. 2016,allthingsliberty.com/2014/06/william-lee-and-oney-judge-a-look-at-george-washington-slavery/.

p.13. "two Waistcoats, and two pair of Breeches . . . nothing of the kind is to be had here." George Washington to Captain Caleb Gibbs, 1 May 1777, *Founders Online.*

p.14. "The servants of the general officers . . . reconnoitered the enemy." Custis, 224.

p.14. "with his usual dignity . . . received the salute." Thacher, 163.

p.14. "Old Billy, Washington's body-servant . . . with great dignity." Lossing, 123.

p.14. "Billy, hand me my horse." Custis, 279.

p.16. "The Mulatto fellow William . . . Lee (the name which he has assumed)." George Washington to Clement Biddle, 28 July 1784, *Founders Online.*

p.17. "revered and beloved . . . every countenance in his presence." Lee, 23.

p.17. "to my utter astonishment . . . private virtue of Washington." Lee, 23.

p.17. "with much difficulty . . . neither Walk, stand, or ride." George Washington Diary, 22 April 1785, *Founders Online.*

p.18. "plain blue coat . . . black breeches and boots." Lee, 28.

p.18. "a clean shirt on . . . white silk stockings." Lee, 28.

p.18. "servant as your old acquaintance Will . . . blacken your shoes." George Washington to David Humphreys, 20 June 1786, *Founders Online.*

p.21. "determined by adding . . . three fifths of all other Persons" "The Constitution of the United States: A Transcription." *National Archives and Records Administration.*

p.21. "at length I have the happiness . . . rising and not a setting Sun." James Madison, *Notes on the Debates in the Federal Convention, Sept 1.*

p.21. "sent my Waiter Will . . . of his other Knee."

George Washington Diary, 1 March 1788, *Founders Online.*

p.22. "Will appears to be . . . well enough to go on." Tobias Lear to Clement Biddle, April 19, 1789, "Selections from the Correspondence of Colonel Clement Biddle." *Pennsylvania Magazine of History and Biography.*

p.22. "continues too bad to remove . . . for a week or two." Clement Biddle to George Washington, 27 April 1789, *Founders Online.*

p.22. "would thank you to propose it to Billy . . . every reasonable wish." Tobias Lear to Clement Biddle, May 3, 1789, "Selections from the Correspondence of Colonel Clement Biddle." *Pennsylvania Magazine of History and Biography.*

p.23. "I shall have a Steel made . . . some Day this Week." Clement Biddle to George Washington, 27 April 1789, *Founders Online.*

p.23. "I hope that Billy . . . New York without accident." Clement Biddle to George Washington, 27 April 1789, *Founders Online,* Note 1.

p.23. "It will be with a heavy expense." Clement Biddle to George Washington, 27 April 1789, *Founders Online,* Note 1.

p.23. "Billy arrived here . . . by his misfortunes." Clement Biddle to George Washington, 27 April 1789, *Founders Online,* Note 1.

p.25. "kept *steadily* to work . . . their business." George Washington to Anthony Whitting, 18 November 1792, *Founders Online.*

p.25. "Mulatto Will should be kept close . . . this business behind." George Washington to William Pearce, 18 May 1794, *Founders Online.*

p.25. "would send his compliments . . . body-servant of the Revolution." Custis, 451.

CHAPTER TWO / Christopher Sheels

p.27. Historians think . . . to July of 1774. Thompson, "The Only Unavoidable Subject of Regret": George Washington, Slavery, and the Enslaved Community at Mount Vernon, 160.

p.32. "Richmond and Christopher . . . yesterday by Water." George Washington to Tobias Lear, 22 November 1790, *Founders Online.*

p.32. "pleased to find by the former that the apprehensions . . . are removed." George Augustine Washington to George Washington, 28 December 1790, *Founders Online.*

p.33. to give directions . . . blacks in this family." Tobias Lear to George Washington, 5 April 1791, *Founders Online.*

p.33. "I know not . . . *yourself & Mrs. Washington.*" George Washington to Tobias Lear, 12 April 1791, *Founders Online.*

p.34. "give no advice . . . to governmental officials." Tobias Lear to George Washington, 24 April 1791, *Founders Online.*

p.34. "use all means to entice them from their masters." Tobias Lear to George Washington, 24 April 1791, *Founders Online.*

p.34. "this will oblige him . . . be next week." Tobias Lear to George Washington, 24 April 1791, *Founders Online.*

p.34. "in a Vessel that sails tomorrow for Alexandria." Tobias Lear to George Washington, 24 April 1791, *Founders Online.*

p.35. "carry them out of the State . . . managed very well." Tobias Lear to George Washington, 24 April 1791, *Founders Online.*

p.35. "You will permit me now . . . state of freedom." Tobias Lear to George Washington, 24 April 1791, *Founders Online.*

p.35. "On Tuesday Mrs Washington . . . children with her & Christopher & Oney." Tobias Lear to George Washington, 15 May 1791, *Founders Online.*

p.36. "On one side . . . if both were forgot." George Washington to Tobias Lear, 9 March 1797, *Founders Online.*

p.37. "supposed to be a little diseased." George Washington to William Stoy, 14 October 1797,

Founders Online.

p.37. "cut out so far as . . . Course of mercury." George Washington to William Stoy, 14 October 1797, *Founders Online.*

p.37. "in a state of Madness" George Washington to William Stoy, 14 October 1797, *Founders Online.*

p.38. "under Your care . . . my own Body servant." George Washington to William Stoy, 14 October 1797, *Founders Online.*

p.38. "in no danger . . . Sheels is Safe." William Stoy to George Washington, 19 October 1797, *Founders Online.*

p.39. "discovery of the Vessel, they contemplate to escape in." George Washington to Roger West, 19 September 1799, *Founders Online.*

p.39-40. "would be equally desirous . . . our cases differ." George Washington to Roger West, 19 September 1799, *Founders Online.*

CHAPTER THREE / Caroline (Branham) & Peter Hardiman

p.41. With the fires beginning to crackle . . . for the next time she emptied them. Glasse, 11-38.

p.44. "Thanks for the Loan of Peter . . . send him Home unhurt." William Fitzhugh to George Washington, 2 November 1785, *Founders Online.*

p.44. "Tarquin has recover'd the Laurells he lost at Alexandria." William Fitzhugh to George Washington, 2 November 1785, *Founders Online.*

p.46. "I have no desire to keep him, if you find a use for him." George Washington to David Stuart, 12 February 1787, *Founders Online.*

p.46. "As you have no immediate occasion . . . unwilling to part with his wife and Children." George Washington to David Stuart, 22 January 1788, *Founders Online.*

p.46. "Caroline is very unwell has had a Smart fever all last week." Anthony Whitting to George Washington, 16 January 1793, *Founders Online.*

p.46. "bled her in the early part of the week . . . hope She will Get better." Anthony Whitting to George Washington, 16 January 1793, *Founders Online.*

p.46. "being in the yard certainly made it more difficult to keep it clean." George Augustine Washington to George Washington, 14 December 1790, *Founders Online*

pp.46-47. "a great number of Negro children . . . doing other mischief." George Washington to William Pearce, 27 October 1793, *Founders Online.*

p.47. "could have tempted me . . . I do not wish to make any profit from it." George Washington Papers, Series 5, Financial Papers: George Washington's Revolutionary War Expense Account, 1775–1783, Library of Congress, https://www.loc.gov/item/mgw500022.

p.48. "I can only repeat to you . . . I am distressed for want of money." George Washington to John Francis Mercer, 8 July 1784, *Founders Online.*

p.48. "If I can sell the Negroes . . . at Publick Sale." Lund Washington to George Washington, 11 March 1778, *Founders Online.*

p.48. "With regard to Sellg the Negroes Mention'd . . . at least for this Summer." Lund Washington to George Washington, 8 April 1778, *Founders Online.*

p.49. "Cash for the Following Negroes. Abram, Orford, Tom, Jack, Ede, Fattimore, Phillis, Bett & Jenny." George Washington Papers, Series 5, Financial Papers: George Washington's Revolutionary War Expense Account, 1775–1783, Library of Congress, https://www.loc.gov/item/mgw500022.

p.49. "I never mean . . . abolished by slow, sure, & imperceptable degrees." George Washington to John Francis Mercer, 9 September 1786, *Founders Online.*

p.49. "With respect to the negroes . . . separation of man and wife, or of families." George Washington to John Francis Mercer, 24 November 1786, *Founders Online.*

p.49. "a generous and noble proof." George Washington to Lafayette, 10 May 1786, *Founders Online.*

p.49. "Would to God a like spirit would . . . by Legislative authority." George Washington to Lafayette, 10 May 1786, *Founders Online.*

p.51. "I have now demands upon me . . . cannot or will not pay it." George Washington to Mary Ball Washington, 15 February 1787, *Founders Online.*

p.51. "Short Crops, & other causes not entirely within my Controul." George Washington to Richard Conway, 4 March 1789, *Founders Online.*

p.51. "what I never expected to . . . borrow money upon interest." George Washington to Richard Conway, 4 March 1789, *Founders Online.*

p.51. On March 6, 1789, Washington . . . paid more than £649. George Washington to Richard Conway, 6 March 1789, *Founders Online,* Note 3.

p.52. "If Peter does *any* work at all . . . do nothing that he can avoid—of labour." George Washington to Anthony Whitting, 4 November 1792, *Founders Online.*

p.52. "I have long suspected that Peter . . . his own pleasures than my benefit." George Washington to Anthony Whitting, 30 December 1792," *Founders Online.*

p.52. "only Six shirts a week . . . under the Overseers thereat." George Washington to Anthony Whitting, 23 December 1792, *Founders Online.*

p.53. "half my Stock may be stolen . . . nothing left to be robbed of." George Washington to Anthony Whitting, 25 November 1792, *Founders Online.*

p.53. "was never celebrated for her honesty . . . it could be done with impunity." George Washington to Anthony Whitting, 17 February 1793, *Founders Online.*

pp.53-54. "it is indispensably necessary . . . find them transgressing these orders." George Washington to Anthony Whitting, 19 May 1793, *Founders Online.*

p.56. "Our horses and the men . . . care of by his domesticks." Staples and Frost, A Day at Mount Vernon in 1797, 9–10.

p.56. "Unless some one pops in . . . set down to dinner by ourselves." George Washington to Tobias Lear, 31 July 1797, *Founders Online.*

p.57. "besides this a ½ doll. for the boy." Lee, 76.

p.58. "Either from habit . . . very good English." Lee, 79.

p.58. "We entered one of the huts of the Blacks . . . some cups and a teapot." Lee, 77–79.

p.58. "I was not a stranger . . . of my linen, of my clothes, etc." Lee, 83.

CHAPTER FOUR / Ona Maria Judge

p.64. "I have not had one half hour to myself since the day of my arrival." Fields, 215.

p.67. "an indulgent master." John Carlile to George Washington, 21 December 1794, *Founders Online.*

p.68. "often complains of not being well . . . does not like to be told so." Fields, 215.

p.68. "Betsy you know is often complaining . . . does not take much pleasure in going out to visit." Fields, 286.

p.70. "Absconded from the household . . . FREDERICK KITT, Steward. May 23" *Encyclopedia of Virginia.* "Advertisement for the Capture of Oney Judge" *Philadelphia Gazette and Universal Daily Advertiser,* May 24, 1796, 1.

p.71. "been the particular attendant on Mrs Washington . . . recover and send her back." George Washington to Oliver Wolcott Jr., 1 September 1796, *Founders Online.*

p.71. "simple and inoffensive." George Washington to Oliver Wolcott Jr., 1 September 1796, *Founders Online.*

p.71. "It is certain the escape has been . . . if it can be avoided." George Washington to Oliver Wolcott Jr., 1 September 1796, *Founders Online.*

p.72. "a thirst for compleat freedom." "Ona Marie Judge," *Weeks Public Library.*

p.72. "she expressed great affection & Reverence . . . sold or given to any other person." "Ona Marie Judge," *Weeks Public Library.*

p.72. "in favor of universal freedom." "Ona Marie Judge," *Weeks Public Library.*

p.72. adopt such measures . . . Constitution of the United States." "Ona Marie Judge," *Weeks Public Library.*

pp.72-73. "To enter into such a compromise . . . far more deserving than herself, of favor." George Washington to Joseph Whipple, 28 November 1796, *Founders Online.*

p.73. "conduct will be forgiven by her Mistress" George Washington to Joseph Whipple, 28 November 1796, *Founders Online.*

p.73. "put on board a Vessel." George Washington to Joseph Whipple, 28 November 1796, *Founders Online.*

p.73. "mean however, by this request . . . in the minds of well disposed Citizens." George Washington to Joseph Whipple, 28 November 1796, *Founders Online.*

p.74. "be a pleasing circumstance to your Aunt." George Washington to Burwell Bassett Jr., 11 August 1799, *Founders Online.*

p.74. "unpleasant, or troublesome" George Washington to Burwell Bassett Jr., 11 August 1799, *Founders Online.*

CHAPTER FIVE / Hercules

p.76. "twenty-five choice SLAVES . . . cattle, sheep, and hogs." The Friends of Freedmen's Cemetery. *Virginia Gazette Items Relating to Slaves in Alexandria and Fairfax County: 1768–1777,* "October 19, 1769 (Rind)."

p.77. "a dark-brown man . . . namesake of fabulous history." Custis, 422.

p.78. "No one need apply who is not perfect . . . to the duties of the station." Decatur, *Private Affairs of George Washington, from the Records and Accounts of Tobias Lear, Esquire, His Secretary,* 93.

p.78. "not from his . . . comes as a Scullion for the Kitchen." George Washington to Tobias Lear, 22 November 1790, *Founders Online.*

p.79. "as highly accomplished a proficient in the culinary art as could be found in the United States." Custis, 422.

p.79. "the whole household, treated the chief cook with much respect . . . good character and pleasing manners." Custis, 422–423.

p.79. "Herculas can answer every purpose . . . she will not." From George Washington to Tobias Lear, 19 June 1791, *Founders Online.*

p.80. "blue cloth coat with velvet collar and bright metal buttons . . . the celebrated dandy." Custis, 423.

p.81. "shone in all his splendor . . . everywhere at the same moment." Custis, 423.

p.82. "Many were not a little surprised on beholding . . . the most polished gentlemen." Custis, 424.

p.82. "nothing can be expected from Richmond . . . no manner of service there." Tobias Lear to George Washington, 1 April 1791, *Founders Online.*

p.82. "intended to send Richmond home . . . willing that he should go." Tobias Lear to George Washington, 17 April 1791, *Founders Online.*

p.82-83. "Richmond goes in a Vessel that sails . . . the best I can think of to accomplish this business." Tobias Lear to George Washington, 24 April 1791, *Founders Online.*

p.83. "go home this week in the Stage . . . make arrangements for his departure." Tobias Lear to George Washington, 22 May 1791, *Founders Online.*

p.83. "was about to go . . . tomorrow takes his departure for Virginia." Tobias Lear to George Washington, 5 June 1791, *Founders Online.*

p.85. "If it shall be found . . . gravel at the place I shewed you." George Washington to James Anderson, 5 November 1796, *Founders Online.*

p.85. "In short let them be employed . . . Keep them

out of idleness & mischief." George Washington to James Anderson, 5 November 1796, *Founders Online.*

p.86. "I hope Richmond was made an example of, for the Robbery he committed on Wilkes Saddle bags." George Washington to William Pearce, 14 November 1796, *Founders Online.*

p.86. "ten dollars & a Quarter that had been stolen by Richmon from James Wlks" Manager Ledger (William Pearce) 1794-1797, 15 November 1796. *Mount Vernon Database for Richmond.*

p.86. "I wish he may not have been put upon it by his father . . . perhaps of a journey together." George Washington to William Pearce, 14 November 1796, *Founders Online.*

p.86. "P.S. What has Frank Herculas & Cyrus been employed in . . . gardeners or other Reports." George Washington to William Pearce, 18 December 1796, *Founders Online.*

p.87. "Herculees absconded." Farm report, 25 February 1797. *Mount Vernon Database for Hercules.*

p.87. "to make all the enquiry he can after Hercules, and send him round in the Vessel if he can be discovered & apprehended." George Washington to Tobias Lear, 10 March 1797, *Founders Online.*

p.87. "said to this little girl that she must be very sad . . . he is free now.'" Lee, 68.

p.87. "unless some particular circumstances should compel me to it." George Washington to John Francis Mercer, 9 September 1786, *Founders Online.*

p.87. "fondness for liquor." Bushrod Washington to George Washington, 8 November 1797, *Founders Online.*

p.87-88. "the running off of my Cook . . . resolution I fear I must break." George Washington to George Lewis, 13 November 1797, *Founders Online.*

p.88. "We have never heard of Herculas . . . he would elude all your vigilance." George Washington to Frederick Kitt, 10 January 1798, *Founders Online.*

p.88. "Since your departure . . . inform you of my success." Frederick Kitt to George Washington, 15 January 1798, *Founders Online.*

CHAPTER SIX / The End of an Era

pp.89-90. "It is demonstratively clear . . . scarcely been able to keep me a float." George Washington to Robert Lewis, 17 August 1799, *Founders Online.*

p.92. Mary V. Thompson, a research historian at Mount Vernon . . . Martha Washington's estate was around £6,055. Thompson, "The Only Unavoidable Subject of Regret": George Washington, Slavery, and the Enslaved Community at Mount Vernon, 865.

p.92. (approximately $647,000 today). Samuel H. Williamson, Seven Ways to Compute the Relative Value of a U.S. Dollar Amount, 1774 to Present, *MeasuringWorth, 2018.*

p.92. "be more tranquil & freer from cares . . . can be defrayed." George Washington to Tobias Lear, 6 May 1794, *Founders Online,* Note 13.

p.93. Thompson estimated . . . people owned by George Washington was around £4,640. Thompson, "The Only Unavoidable Subject of Regret": George Washington, Slavery, and the Enslaved Community at Mount Vernon, 864.

p.93. (approximately $495,000 today). Samuel H. Williamson, Seven Ways to Compute the Relative Value of a U.S. Dollar Amount, 1774 to Present, *MeasuringWorth, 2018.*

p.93. "Upon the decease of my wife . . . to manumit them." Washington, George. *George Washington's will,* Fairfax County, Virginia.

p.94. "I do herby expressly forbid the Sale" Washington, George. *George Washington's wil,* Fairfax County, Virginia.

p.94. "under any pretence whatsoever." Washington, George. *George Washington's will,* Fairfax County, Virginia.

p.94. "And to my Mulatto man William (calling himself William Lee) . . . his faithful services during the Revolutionary War." Washington, George. *George Washington's will.*

p.97. "the remains of the provisions were distributed among the blacks." George Washington, *Letters and Recollections of George Washington: Being Letters to Tobias Lear and others between 1790 and 1799* (London, Archibald Constable and Co., 1906), 141.

p.98. "clear of her negroes & of plantation cares & troubles." Fields, 329.

p.98. Rumors of poison and a possible house fire circulated. Thompson, "The Only Unavoidable Subject of Regret": George Washington, Slavery, and the Enslaved Community at Mount Vernon, 865.

p.99. "Mrs. Washington has announced . . . emancipated. According to the General's wishes." *Spectator* (New York), February 1, 1800, https://lccn.loc.gov/sn83030559.

p.99. "The slaves were left to be emancipated . . . after the general's decease." Custis, 158.

p.99. "Mrs. Washington with all her fortune . . . set them all free at the close of the year." Abigail Adams to Mrs. Richard (Mary) Cranch, December 21, 1800, Massachusetts Historial Society, Adams-Cranch family papers, 1752–1894.

CHAPTER SEVEN / And Then What Happpened?

p.102. "there were about thirty Negroes . . . earnestly after Lord Cornwallis." Sir Augustus John Foster, *Jeffersonian America: Notes on the United States of America Collected in the Years 1805–6–7 and 11–12 by Sir Augustus John Foster, Bart.*, edited by Richard Beale Davis (California: The Huntington Library, 1954), 116–117 (typescript in MVLA Library, Black Research Notebook on "The Tomb").

p.102. "I inquired for the old Slave Servants of the General . . . some inches higher up." Peale, 696.

p.102. "frequently relieved him on such occasions, by bleeding him." Custis, 157.

p.104. "sorry she left Washington . . . made a child of God." Rev. T. H. Adams, "Washington's Runaway Slave and How Portsmouth Freed Her," *Granite Freeman* (Concord, N.H.), May 22, 1845.

p.104. "nearly white, very much freckled . . . maintained as a pauper" Rev. Benjamin Chase, letter to the editor, *The Liberator* (Boston), January 1, 1847.

p.105. "only be managed by one groom, and that always at considerable personal risk." Mason, 175.

p.105. "Upon losing my groom (Peter) . . . I parted with my stock." Mason, *176.*

p.105. After Rachel was freed she had two more children (both free because their mother was free). Thompson, *Slaves on the Mansion Farm*, 61.

p.106. Six days later Costin officially freed Leanthe from slavery. Thompson, *Slaves on the Mansion Farm*, 62.

p.108. "a mulatto, about 44 years old . . . emancipated by R. H. Miller." Provine, 231.

CHAPTER EIGHT / Buried Lives

p.109. "they were a few of the many slaves freed by general George Washington . . . pointed out for them to do." Niles, 187.

pp.110-111. "they were enclosing with a paling . . . training vines over the graves." Joseph A. Downer, "Hallowed Ground, Sacred Place: The Slave Cemetery at George Washington's Mount Vernon and the Cultural Landscapes of the Enslaved" (master's thesis, George Washington University, 2015), 48. *Western Literary Messenger*, 1846:201.

p.112. "I was painfully distressed at the ruin and desolation of the home of Washington . . . a blot on our country!" "Ann Pamela Cunningham," George Washington Digital Encyclopedia, George Washington's Mount Vernon, September 23, 2016, http://www

.mountvernon.org/digital-encyclopedia/article/ann-pamela-cunningham.

p.116."the path the . . . much about it since." Gilliam, Dorothy. "REMEMBRANCE." *Washington Post,* WP Company, 6 February 1982, https://www.washingtonpost.com/archive/local/1982/02/06/remembrance/44ab74fb-0144-4bb2-b22a-2bd93fbf665c/, accessed May 7, 2018.

p.117."This is not about slavery, it's about the strength of the people who endured slavery." Thomas, Pierre. "FORGOTTEN PIONEERS RECALLED AT MOUNT VERNON." *Washington Post,* WP Company, 23 September. 1990, www.washingtonpost.com/archive/local/1990/09/23/forgotten-pioneers-recalled-at-mount-vernon/9df4558f-4d9c-4b0e-87f2-88bc33047108/, accessed May 7, 2018.

p.117."focusing attention on the Slave Memorial at Mount Vernon and . . . the unknown slaves buried there." *House Joint Resolution No. 443, Commemorating the 15th Anniversary of the Slave Memorial at Mount Vernon.* General Assembly of Virginia, 1998 Session, Legislative Information System, https://lis.virginia.gov/cgi-bin/legp604.exe?981+ful+HJ443ER+pdf, accessed May 7, 2018.

p.117."realized the cemetery's grave shafts were amazingly clear, visible just a few inches below the current ground surface." Personal communication with the author.

p.119."We may never know the names of the individuals . . . they go 'unnumbered' no longer." Personal communication with the author.

p.120."recognized for the sacrifices they gave." Personal communication with the author.

p.120."We seek to commemorate the lives . . . locations of individual burial plots." "Videos on Slavery, Slave Memorial Ceremony." *George Washington's Mount Vernon,* Mount Vernon, www.mountvernon.org/george-washington/slavery/.

p.120."unnumbered trailblazers who rest beneath this hallowed space." "Videos on Slavery, Slave Memorial Ceremony." *George Washington's Mount Vernon,* Mount Vernon, www.mountvernon.org/george-washington/slavery/.

p.125."Visible, tangible, and buried in the ground . . . they buried their loved ones." Personal communication with the author.

p.125."tentacles of slavery are reaching from the earth . . . those enslaved at Mount Vernon." Personal communication with the author.

p.126."the power of archaeology . . . enslaved at the plantation." Personal communication with the author.

p.126."It is a profound thing to uncover and identify a grave shaft . . . not possible on other areas of the estate." Green, Nathaniel C. "Uncovering the Past at Mount Vernon's Slave Cemetery." *American Historical Association,* 27 April. 2017, blog.historians.org/2015/07/uncovering-the-past-mount-vernons-slave-cemetery/, accessed May 7, 2018.

p.126."is a direct tangible link to the enslaved community over multiple generations." Personal communication with the author.

p.126."the impact that archaeological fieldwork . . . make a visit more meaningful." Personal communication with the author.

p.126."History belongs to all of us . . . honor the lives of those that made it all possible." Personal communication with the author.

SELECTED BIBLIOGRAPHY

BOOKS

Blassingame, John W. *Slave Testimony: Two Centuries of Letters, Speeches, Interviews, and Autobiographies.* Baton Rouge: LSU Press, 1977.

Bradburn, Douglas and John C. Coombs. *Early Modern Virginia: Reconsidering the Old Dominion.* Charlottesville: Univ. of Virginia, 2011.

Custis, George Washington Parke, Mary Randolph Custis Lee, and Benson John Lossing. *Recollections and Private Memoirs of Washington.* New York: Derby & Jackson, 1860.

Dann, John C. *The Revolution Remembered: Eyewitness Accounts of the War for Independence.* Chicago: Univ. of Chicago, 1980, pp. 408-409.

Decatur, Stephen, and Tobias Lear. *Private Affairs of George Washington, from the Records and Accounts of Tobias Lear, Esquire, His Secretary.* Boston: Houghton Mifflin, 1933.

Fields, Joseph E. *Worthy Partner: The Papers of Martha Washington.* Westport, CT: Greenwood, 1994.

Foster, Sir Augustus John. *Jeffersonian America: Notes on the United States of America Collected in the Years 1805–7 and 1811–12,* edited by Richard Beale Davis (California: The Huntington Library, 1954), pp. 116–117 (typescript in MVLA Library, Black Research Notebook on "The Tomb").

Glasse, Hannah. *The Servant's Directory, Or, House-keeper's Companion: Wherein the Duties of the Chamber-maid, Nursery-maid, House-maid, Landery-maid, Scullion or Under-cook Are Fully and Distinctly Explained, to Which Is Annexed a Diary or House-keeper's Pocket-book for the Whole Year, with Directions for Keeping Accounts with Tradesmen, and Many Other Particulars Fit to Be Known by the Mistress of a Family.* London: Printed for the Author and Sold by W. Johnston . . . at Mrs. Ashburnham's China-shop . . . Mr. Vaughn's . . . and by All the Booksellers in Town and Country, 1760.

Hirschfeld, Fritz. *George Washington and Slavery: a Documentary Portrayal.* Columbia, Mo.: Univ. of Missouri, 1997.

Humphreys, David, *Life of General Washington,* edited by Rosemarie Zagarri (Athens: University of Georgia Press, 1991), p. 78.

Kotar, S. L., and J. E. Gessler. *The Rise of the American Circus, 1716–1899.* Jefferson, NC: McFarland, 2011. pp. 55–58.

Lee, Jean Butenhoff. *Experiencing Mount Vernon: Eyewitness Accounts, 1784–1865.* Charlottesville: Univ. of Virginia, 2006.

Lossing, Benson J. *Hours With the Living Men and Women of the Revolution: A Pilgrimage.* New York: Funk & Wagnalls, 1889, p.123.

Mason, Richard. *The Gentleman's New Pocket Farrier, Comprising a General Description of the Noble and Useful Animal the Horse* Philadelphia: Grigg & Elliot, 1844, p.175.

Morgan, Edmund S. *American Slavery, American Freedom: The Ordeal of Colonial Virginia.* New York: Norton, 1975.

Niles, Hezekiah, ed., *Niles' Weekly Register,* Vol.

XLIX (Baltimore: n.p., n.d), p. 187.
Peale, Charles Willson, Lillian B. Miller, Sidney Hart, David C. Ward, and Toby A. Appel. *The Selected Papers of Charles Willson Peale and His Family.* 2nd ed. Vol. 2. New Haven: Yale University Press, 1983, p. 696.
Pogue, Dennis J. *Founding Spirits: George Washington and the Beginnings of the American Whiskey Industry.* Buena Vista: Harbour Books, 2014.
Provine, Dorothy S., abstractor and indexer, *Alexandria County, Virginia, Free Negro Registers, 1797–1861* Bowie, MD: Heritage Books, Inc., 1990.
Schwarz, Philip J. *Slavery at the Home of George Washington.* Mount Vernon, Va.: Mount Vernon Ladies' Association, 2001.
Staples, Hamilton B. and Amariah Frost. *A Day at Mount Vernon in 1797,* A paper read before the American Antiquarian Society at their semi-annual meeting in Boston, April 30, 1879, by Hamilton B. Staples. Privately printed.
Thacher, James, and Samuel X. Radbill. *Military Journal of the American Revolution: From the Commencement to the Disbanding of the American Army: Comprising a Detailed Account of the Principal Events and Battles of the Revolution with Their Exact Dates, and a Biographical Sketch of the Most Prominent Generals.* Hartford, CT: Hurlbut, Williams, 1862, p. 163.
Thompson, Mary V. "*The Only Unavoidable Subject of Regret": George Washington, Slavery, and the Enslaved Community at Mount Vernon.* (Pending publication, 2019, Univ. of Virginia Press)
Louis-Phillippe, *Journal de mon voyage d'Amérique,* trans. Ormonde de Kay, Jr. (Mount Vernon archives.)

LETTERS

Abigail Adams to Mrs. Richard (Mary) Cranch, December 21, 1800, Massachusetts Historical Society, Adams-Cranch family papers, 1752–1894.

ARTICLES

Adams, Rev. T. H., "Washington's Runaway Slave and How Portsmouth Freed Her," *Granite Freeman* (Concord, N.H.), May 22, 1845.
Chase, Rev. Benjamin, letter to the editor, *The Liberator* (Boston), January 1, 1847.

ONLINE DATABASES

"Estimates," Voyages: The Trans-Atlantic Slave Trade Database, Emory University, accessed February 13, 2018, http://www.slavevoyages.org/assessment/estimates.
Mount Vernon, Digital Humanities Research (ongoing, unpublished original research from primary source documents housed at Mount Vernon). Individual files on the following enslaved people: William Lee, Caroline, Christopher Sheels, Delia, Delphy, Doll, Frank Lee, Hercules, Lucy C., Lucy D., Marcus, Nathan A., Oney Judge, Peter Hardiman, Richmond, and Suckey Bay.

ONLINE ARTICLES

Baumgarten, Linda. *Journal of Early Southern American Arts.* The Museum of Early Southern American Arts, 1 November 1988. Web. 4 Jan. 2016.
Gilliam, Dorothy. "REMEMBRANCE." *Washington Post,* WP Company, 6 Feb. 1982, https://www.washingtonpost.com/archive/local/1982/02/06/remembrance/44ab74fb-0144-4bb2-b22a-2bd93fbf665c/ Web, accessed May 7, 2018.
"Founders Online: Advertisement for Runaway Slaves, 11 August 1761." Advertisement for Runaway Slaves, 11 August 1761. Web. 30 Dec. 2015. http://founders.archives.gov/documents/Washington/02-07-02-0038.
"Letters and Recollections of George Washington." Google Books. N.p., n.d. Web. 23 Sept. 2016. p. 141.
House Joint Resolution No. 443, Commemorating

the 15th anniversary of the Slave Memorial at Mount Vernon. General Assembly of Virginia, 1998 Session, Legislative Information System, https://lis.virginia.gov/cgi-bin/legp604.exe?981+ful+HJ443ER+pdf, accessed May 7, 2018.

Madison, James. "Avalon Project—Madison Debates — September 17." N.p., n.d. Web. 21 Sept. 2016. http://avalon.law.yale.edu/18th_century/debates_917.asp#24

"Oney Judge." George Washington's Mount Vernon. Web. 30 Dec. 2015. http://www.mountvernon.org/research-collections/digital-encyclopedia/article/oney-judge/.

"Ona Maria Judge." Weeks Public Library. Web 22 Sept. 2016. http://www.weekslibrary.org/ona_maria_judge.htm

Pierre, Thomas. "Forgotten Pioneers Recalled At Mount Vernon." *Washington Post*, WP Company, 23 Sept. 1990, www.washingtonpost.com/archive/local/1990/09/23/forgotten-pioneers-recalled-at-mount-vernon/9df4558f-4d9c-4b0e-87f2-88bc33047108/, accessed May 7, 2018.

"The Spectator." (New York, NY), February 1, 1800, page 3 Library of Congress LCCN Permalink for Sn83030559. N.p., n.d. Web. 23 Sept. 2016. https://lccn.loc.gov/sn83030559.

"The President's House in Historic Philadelphia." Ushistory.org. Independence Hall Association. Web. 30 Dec. 2015. http://www.ushistory.org/presidentshouse/.

Thompson, Mary V. "William Lee & Oney Judge: A Look at George Washington & Slavery | Journal of the American Revolution." *Journal of the American Revolution.* 2014. Web. 18 Feb. 2016. http://allthingsliberty.com/2014/06/william-lee-and-oney-judge-a-look-at-george-washington-slavery/.

Thompson, Mary V. "The Only Unavoidable Subject of Regret" George Washington's Mount Vernon. "List of George Washington's Slaves, 1799." Papers of George Washington. Web. 3 Nov. 2015. http://gwpapers.virginia.edu/documents/list-of-george-washingtons-slaves-1799/.

Thompson, Mary V. "The Private Lives of George Washington's Slaves." PBS. PBS. Web. 3 Nov. 2015. http://www.pbs.org/wgbh/pages/frontline/shows/jefferson/video/lives.html.

"Transcriptions of Virginia Gazette Runaway Slave Ads." Transcriptions of Virginia Gazette Runaway Slave Ads. Web. 2 Feb. 2015. http://teachers.history.org/resources/lesson-plans/attitudes-and-behaviors-regarding-slavery-during-colonial-period/transcription.

Twohig, By Dorothy. "That Species of Property": Washington's Role in the Controversy Over Slavery - The Washington Papers." The Washington Papers. N.p., n.d. Web. 12 Sept. 2016.

ONLINE SOURCES

Encyclopedia of Virginia. "Advertisement for the Capture of Oney Judge" *Philadelphia Gazette* and *Universal Daily Advertiser*, May 24, 1796, 1. https://www.encyclopediavirginia.org/Advertisement_for_the_Capture_of_Oney_Judge_Philadelphia_Gazette_May_24_1796, accessed May 1, 2018.

The Friends of Freedmen's Cemetery. "October 19, 1769 (Rind)." Virginia Gazette Items Relating to Slaves in Alexandria and Fairfax County: 1768–1777, last modified April 29, 2007. www.freedmenscemetery.org/resources/documents/1768vagazette.shtml accessed May 1, 2018.

"The Constitution of the United States: A Transcription." National Archives and Records Administration, last reviewed October 23, 2017, https://www.archives.gov/founding-docs/constitution-transcript

James Madison, Notes on the Debates in the Federal Convention, Sept 17, Avalon Project, http://avalon.law.yale.edu/18th_century/debates_917.asp#24.

George Washington Digital Encyclopedia. "Ann Pamela Cunningham," George Washington's Mount Vernon, September 23, 2016, http://www.mountvernon.org/digital-encyclopedia/article/ann-pamela-cunningham.

George Washington Papers, Series 5, Financial Papers: George Washington's Revolutionary War Expense Account, 1775–1783, Library of Congress, https://www.loc.gov/item/mgw500022.

George Washington's will, Fairfax County Virginia. https://www.fairfaxcounty.gov/circuit/sites/circuit/files/assets/documents/pdf/george-washington-will.pdf, accessed March 14, 2018.

Green, Nathaniel C. "Uncovering the Past at Mount Vernon's Slave Cemetery." American Historical Association, 27 Apr. 2017, blog.historians.org/2015/07/uncovering-the-past-mount-vernons-slave-cemetery/, accessed May 7, 2018.

Letter from Tobias Lear to Clement Biddle, April 19, 1789, "Selections from the Correspondence of Colonel Clement Biddle (continued)," *Pennsylvania Magazine of History and Biography,* Vol. 43, No. 1 (n.p., University of Pennsylvania Press, 1919), 60, http://www.jstor.org/stable/pdf/20086366.pdf.

Letter from Tobias Lear to Clement Biddle, May 3, 1789, "Selections from the Correspondence of Colonel Clement Biddle (continued)," *Pennsylvania Magazine of History and Biography,* Vol. 43, No. 1 (n.p., University of Pennsylvania Press, 1919), 61–62, http://www.jstor.org/stable/pdf/20086366.pdf.

Samuel H. Williamson, Seven Ways to Compute the Relative Value of a U.S. Dollar Amount, 1774 to Present, MeasuringWorth, 2018." Measuring Worth. Accessed March 14, 2018. https://www.measuringworth.com/calculators/uscompare/.

FOUNDERS ONLINE

"From George Washington to John Francis Mercer, 9 September 1786," Founders Online, National Archives, last modified April 12, 2018, http://founders.archives.gov/documents/Washington/04-04-02-0232.

"From George Washington to Captain Caleb Gibbs, 1 May 1777," Founders Online, National Archives, last modified April 12, 2018, http://founders.archives.gov/documents/Washington/03-09-02-0306.

"From George Washington to Clement Biddle, 28 July 1784," Founders Online, National Archives, last modified April 12, 2018, http://founders.archives.gov/documents/Washington/04-02-02-0014.

"[Diary entry: 22 April 1785]," Founders Online, National Archives, last modified April 12, 2018, http://founders.archives.gov/documents/Washington/01-04-02-0002-0004-0022.

"From George Washington to David Humphreys, 20 June 1786," Founders Online, National Archives, last modified April 12, 2018, http://founders.archives.gov/documents/Washington/04-04-02-0117.

"[Diary entry: 1 March 1788]," Founders Online, National Archives, last modified April 12, 2018, http://founders.archives.gov/documents/Washington/01-05-02-0004-0003-0001.

"To George Washington from Clement Biddle, 27 April 1789," Founders Online, National Archives, last modified April 12, 2018, http://founders.archives.gov/documents/Washington/05-02-02-0115.

"To George Washington from Clement Biddle, 27 April 1789," Founders Online, National Archives, last modified April 12, 2018, http://founders.archives.gov/documents/Washington/05-02-02-0115.

"From George Washington to Anthony Whitting, 18 November 1792," Founders Online, National Archives, last modified April 12, 2018, http://founders.archives.gov/documents/Washington/05-11-02-0228.

"From George Washington to William Pearce,

18 May 1794," Founders Online, National Archives, last modified April 12, 2018, http://founders.archives.gov/documents/Washington/05-16-02-0073.
"From George Washington to Tobias Lear, 22 November 1790," Founders Online, National Archives, last modified April 12, 2018, http://founders.archives.gov/documents/Washington/05-06-02-0331.
"To George Washington from George Augustine Washington, 28 December 1790," Founders Online, National Archives, last modified April 12, 2018, http://founders.archives.gov/documents/Washington/05-07-02-0078.
"To George Washington from Tobias Lear, 5 April 1791," Founders Online, National Archives, last modified April 12, 2018, http://founders.archives.gov/documents/Washington/05-08-02-0050.
"From George Washington to Tobias Lear, 12 April 1791," Founders Online, National Archives, last modified April 12, 2018, http://founders.archives.gov/documents/Washington/05-08-02-0062.
"To George Washington from Tobias Lear, 24 April 1791," Founders Online, National Archives, last modified April 12, 2018, http://founders.archives.gov/documents/Washington/05-08-02-0099.
"To George Washington from Tobias Lear, 15 May 1791," Founders Online, National Archives, last modified April 12, 2018, http://founders.archives.gov/documents/Washington/05-08-02-0148.
"From George Washington to Tobias Lear, 9 March 1797," Founders Online, National Archives, last modified April 12, 2018, http://founders.archives.gov/documents/Washington/06-01-02-0017.
"From George Washington to William Stoy, 14 October 1797," Founders Online, National Archives, last modified April 12, 2018, http://founders.archives.gov/documents/Washington/06-01-02-0360.
"To George Washington from William Stoy, 19 October 1797," Founders Online, National Archives, last modified April 12, 2018, http://founders.archives.gov/documents/Washington/06-01-02-0369.
"From George Washington to Roger West, 19 September 1799," Founders Online, National Archives, last modified April 12, 2018, http://founders.archives.gov/documents/Washington/06-04-02-0262.
"To George Washington from William Fitzhugh, 2 November 1785," Founders Online, National Archives, last modified April 12, 2018, http://founders.archives.gov/documents/Washington/04-03-02-0300.
"From George Washington to David Stuart, 12 February 1787," Founders Online, National Archives, last modified April 12, 2018, http://founders.archives.gov/documents/Washington/04-05-02-0022.
"From George Washington to David Stuart, 22 January 1788," Founders Online, National Archives, last modified April 12, 2018, http://founders.archives.gov/documents/Washington/04-06-02-0045.
"To George Washington from Anthony Whitting, 16 January 1793," Founders Online, National Archives, last modified April 12, 2018, http://founders.archives.gov/documents/Washington/05-12-02-0005.
"To George Washington from George Augustine Washington, 14 December 1790," Founders Online, National Archives, last modified April 12, 2018, http://founders.archives.gov/documents/Washington/05-07-02-0042.
"From George Washington to William Pearce, 27 October 1793," Founders Online, National Archives, last modified April 12, 2018, http://founders.archives.gov/documents/Washington/05-14-02-0210.
"From George Washington to John Francis Mercer, 8 July 1784," Founders Online, National Archives, last modified April 12, 2018,

http://founders.archives.gov/documents/Washington/04-01-02-0348.
"To George Washington from Lund Washington, 11 March 1778," Founders Online, National Archives, last modified April 12, 2018, http://founders.archives.gov/documents/Washington/03-14-02-0117.
"To George Washington from Lund Washington, 8 April 1778," Founders Online, National Archives, last modified April 12, 2018, http://founders.archives.gov/documents/Washington/03-14-02-0410.
"From George Washington to John Francis Mercer, 9 September 1786," Founders Online, National Archives, last modified April 12, 2018, http://founders.archives.gov/documents/Washington/04-04-02-0232.
"From George Washington to John Francis Mercer, 24 November 1786," Founders Online, National Archives, last modified April 12, 2018, http://founders.archives.gov/documents/Washington/04-04-02-0353.
"From George Washington to Lafayette, 10 May 1786," Founders Online, National Archives, last modified April 12, 2018, http://founders.archives.gov/documents/Washington/04-04-02-0051.
"From George Washington to Mary Ball Washington, 15 February 1787," Founders Online, National Archives, last modified April 12, 2018, http://founders.archives.gov/documents/Washington/04-05-02-0030.
"From George Washington to Richard Conway, 4 March 1789," Founders Online, National Archives, last modified April 12, 2018, http://founders.archives.gov/documents/Washington/05-01-02-0272.
"From George Washington to Richard Conway, 6 March 1789," Founders Online, National Archives, last modified April 12, 2018, http://founders.archives.gov/documents/Washington/05-01-02-0279.
"From George Washington to Anthony Whitting, 4 November 1792," Founders Online, National Archives, last modified April 12, 2018, http://founders.archives.gov/documents/Washington/05-11-02-0182.
"From George Washington to Anthony Whitting, 30 December 1792," Founders Online, National Archives, last modified April 12, 2018, http://founders.archives.gov/documents/Washington/05-11-02-0355.
"From George Washington to Anthony Whitting, 23 December 1792," Founders Online, National Archives, last modified April 12, 2018, http://founders.archives.gov/documents/Washington/05-11-02-0336.
"From George Washington to Anthony Whitting, 25 November 1792," Founders Online, National Archives, last modified April 12, 2018, http://founders.archives.gov/documents/Washington/05-11-02-0251.
"From George Washington to Anthony Whitting, 17 February 1793," Founders Online, National Archives, last modified April 12, 2018, http://founders.archives.gov/documents/Washington/05-12-02-0116.
"From George Washington to Anthony Whitting, 19 May 1793," Founders Online, National Archives, last modified April 12, 2018, http://founders.archives.gov/documents/Washington/05-12-02-0483.
"From George Washington to Tobias Lear, 31 July 1797," Founders Online, National Archives, last modified April 12, 2018, http://founders.archives.gov/documents/Washington/06-01-02-0239.
"To George Washington from John Carlile, 21 December 1794," Founders Online, National Archives, last modified April 12, 2018, http://founders.archives.gov/documents/Washington/05-17-02-0207.
"From George Washington to Oliver Wolcott, Jr., 1 September 1796," Founders Online, National

Archives, last modified April 12, 2018, http://founders.archives.gov/documents/Washington/99-01-02-00910. [This is an Early Access document from The Papers of George Washington. It is not an authoritative final version.]

"From George Washington to Oliver Wolcott, Jr., 1 September 1796," Founders Online, National Archives, last modified April 12, 2018, http://founders.archives.gov/documents/Washington/99-01-02-00910. [This is an Early Access document from The Papers of George Washington. It is not an authoritative final version.]

"From George Washington to Joseph Whipple, 28 November 1796," Founders Online, National Archives, last modified April 12, 2018, http://founders.archives.gov/documents/Washington/99-01-02-00037. [This is an Early Access document from The Papers of George Washington. It is not an authoritative final version.]

"From George Washington to Burwell Bassett, Jr., 11 August 1799," Founders Online, National Archives, last modified April 12, 2018, http://founders.archives.gov/documents/Washington/06-04-02-0197.

"From George Washington to Tobias Lear, 22 November 1790," Founders Online, National Archives, last modified April 12, 2018, http://founders.archives.gov/documents/Washington/05-06-02-0331.

"From George Washington to Tobias Lear, 19 June 1791," Founders Online, National Archives, last modified April 12, 2018, http://founders.archives.gov/documents/Washington/05-08-02-0193.

"To George Washington from Tobias Lear, 1 April 1791," Founders Online, National Archives, last modified April 12, 2018, http://founders.archives.gov/documents/Washington/05-08-02-0027.

"To George Washington from Tobias Lear, 17 April 1791," Founders Online, National Archives, last modified April 12, 2018, http://founders.archives.gov/documents/Washington/05-08-02-0090.

"To George Washington from Tobias Lear, 24 April 1791," Founders Online, National Archives, last modified April 12, 2018, http://founders.archives.gov/documents/Washington/05-08-02-0099.

"To George Washington from Tobias Lear, 22 May 1791," Founders Online, National Archives, last modified April 12, 2018, http://founders.archives.gov/documents/Washington/05-08-02-0156.

"To George Washington from Tobias Lear, 5 June 1791," Founders Online, National Archives, last modified April 12, 2018, http://founders.archives.gov/documents/Washington/05-08-02-0172.

"From George Washington to James Anderson, 5 November 1796," Founders Online, National Archives, last modified April 12, 2018, http://founders.archives.gov/documents/Washington/99-01-02-01064. [This is an Early Access document from The Papers of George Washington. It is not an authoritative final version.]

"From George Washington to James Anderson, 5 November 1796," Founders Online, National Archives, last modified April 12, 2018, http://founders.archives.gov/documents/Washington/99-01-02-01064. [This is an Early Access document from The Papers of George Washington. It is not an authoritative final version.]

"From George Washington to William Pearce, 14 November 1796," Founders Online, National Archives, last modified April 12, 2018, http://founders.archives.gov/documents/Washington/99-01-02-00003. [This is an Early Access document from The Papers of George Washington. It is not an authoritative final version.]

"From George Washington to William Pearce, 18 December 1796," Founders Online, National Archives, last modified April 12, 2018,

http://founders.archives.gov/documents/Washington/99-01-02-00102. [This is an Early Access document from The Papers of George Washington. It is not an authoritative final version.]
"From George Washington to Tobias Lear, 10 March 1797," Founders Online, National Archives, last modified April 12, 2018, http://founders.archives.gov/documents/Washington/06-01-02-0019.
"From George Washington to John Francis Mercer, 9 September 1786," Founders Online, National Archives, last modified April 12, 2018, http://founders.archives.gov/documents/Washington/04-04-02-0232.
"To George Washington from Bushrod Washington, 8 November 1797," Founders Online, National Archives, last modified April 12, 2018, http://founders.archives.gov/documents/Washington/06-01-02-0414.
"From George Washington to George Lewis, 13 November 1797," Founders Online, National Archives, last modified April 12, 2018, http://founders.archives.gov/documents/Washington/06-01-02-0419.
"From George Washington to Frederick Kitt, 10 January 1798," Founders Online, National Archives, last modified April 12, 2018, http://founders.archives.gov/documents/Washington/06-02-02-0016.
"To George Washington from Frederick Kitt, 15 January 1798," Founders Online, National Archives, last modified April 12, 2018, http://founders.archives.gov/documents/Washington/06-02-02-0026.
"From George Washington to Robert Lewis, 17 August 1799," Founders Online, National Archives, last modified April 12, 2018, http://founders.archives.gov/documents/Washington/06-04-02-0211.
"From George Washington to Tobias Lear, 6 May 1794," Founders Online, National Archives, last modified April 12, 2018, http://founders.archives.gov/documents/Washington/05-16-02-0023.

LECTURES

Thompson, Mary V. "Different People, Different Stories: The Life Stories of Individual Slaves from Mount Vernon and Their Relationships with George and Martha Washington." George Washington and Slavery. George Washington's Mount Vernon, Mount Vernon. 3 Nov. 2001.
Thompson, Mary V. "William Lee and Oney Judge: A Look at George Washington & Slavery through the Biographies of Two Enslaved Residents of Mount Vernon." George Washington Society, New Castle, Delaware. 7 June 2015.

UNPUBLISHED RESEARCH PAPERS

Downer, Joseph A. "Hallowed Ground, Sacred Place: The Slave Cemetery at George Washington's Mount Vernon and the Cultural Landscapes of the Enslaved." Web. 30 Dec. 2015, p. 48. http://www.academia.edu/10928187/Hallowed_Ground_Sacred_Place_The_Slave_Cemetery_At_George_Washington_s_Mount_Vernon_And_The_Cultural_Landscapes_Of_The_Enslaved.
Thompson, Mary V. Information on Mount Vernon Slaves Who Died, Were Sold, or Escaped Prior to the Summer of 1799 and the Compilation of George Washington's Final Slave List. Mount Vernon: Mount Vernon Ladies' Association, 2005.
Thompson, Mary V. Slaves on the Dogue Run Farm-1799. Mount Vernon: Mount Vernon Ladies' Association, 1992, 1997, 2003, and 2014.
Thompson, Mary V. Slaves on the Muddy Hole Farm-1799. Mount Vernon: Mount Vernon Ladies' Association, 1992, 1997, 2003, and 2014.
Thompson, Mary V. Slaves on the River Farm—1799. Mount Vernon: Mount Vernon Ladies' Association, 1992, 1997, 2005, and 2014.
Thompson, Mary V. Slaves on the Union Farm-

1799. Mount Vernon: Mount Vernon Ladies' Association, 1992, 1997, 2003, and 2014.

Thompson, Mary V. That Hospitable Mansion: Hospitality at George Washington's Mount Vernon. Mount Vernon: Mount Vernon Ladies' Association, 2003, 2004, 2005, 2014. U

INTERVIEWS IN PERSON WITH AUTHOR

Breen, Eleanor, October 29, 2013, November 14, 2014.

Coates, Sheila, August 24, 2017.

Downer, Joe, January 20, 2016.

Kerr, Molly, January 28, 2016.

MacLeod, Jessie, January 20, 2016.

Miller-Matema, ZSun-nee, August 27, 2017.

Price, Karen, January 20, 2016.

Parker, Brenda, January 28, 2016.

Quander, Judge Rohulamin, January 21, 2016.

Quander, Jay, January 28, 2016.

White, Esther, October 29, 2013.

INTERVIEWS BY PHONE WITH AUTHOR

Bakari, Harvey, February 12, 2016.

Breen, Dr. Eleanor, November 10, 2015.

Kerr, Molly, November 11, 2015.

MacLeod, Jessie, November 13, 2015.

Miller-Matema, ZSun-nee, February 3, 2016.

White, Esther, June 19, 2017

VIDEOS

"Videos on Slavery, Slave Memorial Ceremony." George Washington's Mount Vernon, Mount Vernon, www.mountvernon.org/george-washington/slavery/.

PICTURE CREDITS

Courtesy of Hon. John T. Frey, Clerk, Fairfax Circuit Court: p. 95

Courtesy of Independence National Historical Park: p. 21

Courtesy of Mount Vernon Ladies' Association: title page, pp. 12, 13, 19, 23, 24, 26 (top and bottom), 28, 37, 42, 45, 50, 55 (bottom), 57, 64, 75, 77, 78, 84, 91, 98, 100, 108, 113 (top and bottom), 115, 116 (left and right), 118, 119, 121 (top and bottom), 122, 123, 124, 125, 128, 129, 130

Courtesy of the Maryland Historical Society: p. 55 (top)

Courtesy of the National Park Service: p. 105 (bottom)

Courtesy of Private Collection: p. 81

Library of Congress: pp. 2 (middle), 2-3 (top detail of middle image), 60, 80, 107 (top)

Metropolitan Museum of Art: p. 15

National Gallery of Art: p.31

New York Public Library Digital Collections: pp. 62, 63

Special Collections, John D. Rockefeller Jr. Library, The Colonial Williamsburg Foundation: pp. 2 (bottom), 39

The *Pennsylvania Gazette*, May 24, 1796: p. 70

ACKNOWLEDGMENTS

I'd like to thank my excellent editor at Holiday House, Kelly Loughman, for her sensitive, thoughtful insights, and her commitment to this topic. She has been a joy to work with as we have discussed at length every detail of this book—more than once. I appreciate Kelly's unfailing confidence in me throughout the process.

For the past 160 years, the Mount Vernon Ladies Association (MVLA) has owned and operated George Washington's Mount Vernon—without federal funding. I am grateful to these women, both past and present, who had the foresight to protect and preserve this treasure of American history. For her encouragement for this book, I'd especially like to thank Cathy Mayton, the MVLA Vice Regent for Arkansas.

This book would not have been possible without the assistance of many staff members at Mount Vernon who have helped me in countless ways. I'm grateful for the friendship of Diana Cordray, Manager of the Education Center, and her husband, Dennis, who have welcomed me with open arms and open hearts every time I've visited Mount Vernon. My deepest appreciation goes to Mary V. Thompson, the amazing research historian, who answered hundreds of my questions, generously shared with me her vast knowledge of all things Washington, and reviewed the entire book for historical accuracy. Many thanks go to Dawn Bonner, Manager of Visual Resources, who—cheerfully without fail—repeatedly supplied me with the images and information I needed. I am grateful to Molly Kerr, former Mount Vernon Digital Humanities Program Manager, who compiled a comprehensive database on the enslaved population taken from primary source documents. Access to this database was of utmost importance as I learned as much as possible about the individuals I featured in this book.

A special thank-you goes to Dr. Esther White and Dr. Eleanor Breen, both former archaeologists at Mount Vernon. The inspiration for this book came as a result of a conversation I had with them. They shared their plans with me for the Slave Cemetery Archaeological Survey. Their passion and excitement over what could be learned from this archaeological dig was contagious—and the idea for this book was born. I'd also like to thank Luke Pecoraro, Director of Archeology, and Joe A. Downer, Archaeological Crew Chief, who have shared this ongoing work with me. Joe has answered my many questions, shared photos with me, and allowed me to join his team for a couple of days to work in the cemetery dig site. I also appreciate Sean

Devlin, curator of Archeological Collections, for answering my questions about artifacts.

Many others at Mount Vernon have helped me in a variety of ways. My thanks go to Dr. Doug Bradburn, President and CEO; Carol Cadou, former Senior Vice President, Historic Preservation & Collections; Dr. Susan P. Schoelwer, Robert H. Smith Senior Curator; Jessie MacLeod, Assistant Curator; Allison Wickens, Vice President, Education; and Brenda Parker, a first-person interpreter who gracefully portrays Caroline Branham, one of the enslaved women featured in this book. Many other staff members—too numerous to name—have helped me in countless large and small ways for which I am grateful.

I am also grateful for the assistance of several people at The Colonial Williamsburg Foundation. Thank you Doug Mayo, Associate Librarian, and Marianne Martin, Visual Resources Librarian, John D. Rockefeller Jr. Library, for helping me with images and for giving us permission to create silhouettes based on their photos, which grace the front cover. I also appreciate Harvey Bakari, Colonial Williamsburg's Manager of African American Initiatives who shared his knowledge with me.

I'd also like to thank Heather Bollinger, Historic Records Manager, Fairfax Circuit Court Historic Records Center for her assistance. I am deeply grateful to Coxey Toogood for generously sharing her beautiful historic art.

I am grateful to Kimberly Wallace-Sanders, PhD, Associate Professor of American Cultural History and African American Studies, Emory University, for her insightful sensitivity read of *Buried Lives*. Dr. Wallace-Sanders's thoughtful feedback informed my writing in invaluable ways.

I appreciate the help of Sheila Coates, founder and president of Black Women United for Action, who works with Mount Vernon each year to host a remembrance ceremony to recognize the contributions of the enslaved community who lived, worked, and died there.

One part of my research was interviewing descendants of some of the people who were enslaved at Mount Vernon during George Washington's lifetime. My gratitude goes to ZSun-nee Miller-Matema, a descendant of Caroline Branham, who worked as a housemaid. ZSun-nee not only shared her family history with me but graciously agreed to write the forward for this book. Several other descendants took time to visit with me in person or by phone, which was a great treat for me. I am deeply grateful to each of the following people for sharing their ancestors with me: Judge Rohulamin Quander and Jay Quander, both descendants of Suckey Bay; Shawn Costly, descendant of Davy and Edy Jones; Ann Chinn, descendant of George and Sall Twine; Phyllis Ford, descendant of Dick and Charity Jasper; and Stephen Hammond, descendant of Nancy Syphax.

Index

Page numbers in italics refer to photographs and illustrations in the text

N

P

Q

R

S

T

U